FENCE
BOOKS

THE NATIONAL POETRY SERIES was established in 1978 to ensure the publication of five poetry books annually through five participating publishers. Publication is funded annually by the Lannan Foundation, Amazon Literary Partnership, Barnes & Noble, The Poetry Foundation, The PG Family Foundation and The Betsy Community Fund, Joan Bingham, Mariana Cook, Stephen Graham, Juliet Lea Hillman Simonds, William Kistler, Jeffrey Ravetch, Laura Baudo Sillerman, and Margaret Thornton.

For a complete listing of generous contributors to The National Poetry Series, please visit WWW.NATIONALPOETRYSERIES.ORG.

2014 COMPETITION WINNERS

MONOGRAPH

by Simeon Berry of Somerville, MA
Chosen by Denise Duhamel for University of Georgia Press

THE REGRET HISTORIES

by Joshua Poteat of Richmond, VA
Chosen by Campbell McGrath for HarperCollins

LET'S LET THAT ARE NOT YET : INFERNO

by Ed Pavlić of Athens, GA
Chosen by John Keene for Fence Books

DOUBLE JINX

by Nancy Reddy of Madison, WI
Chosen by Alex Lemon for Milkweed Editions

VIABILITY

by Sarah Vap of Venice, CA
Chosen by Mary Jo Bang for Penguin Books

Let's Let That
   Are Not Yet :

INFERNO

Published in the United States by Fence Books, Science Library 320,
University of Albany, 1400 Washington Avenue, Albany, NY 12222

www.fenceportal.org

Fence Books are distributed by Consortium Book Sales & Distribution (cbsd.com) and Small
Press Distribution (spdbooks.org).

Book design by Jess Puglisi

Library of Congress Cataloging in Publication Data
Pavlić, Ed [1966-]
Let's Let That Are Not Yet: Inferno/ Ed Pavlić
Library of Congress Control Number: 2015950578

ISBN-13 978-1934200964

FIRST EDITION
10 9 8 7 6 5 4 3 2

Fence Books are published in partnership with the University at Albany and the New York State
Writers Institute, and with help from the New York State Council on the Arts and the National
Endowment for the Arts and the Fence Trust.

Let's Let That
Are Not Yet :

INFERNO

NATIONAL POETRY SERIES
SELECTED BY **JOHN KEENE**

Ed Pavlić

For Milan

...a kind of theater focused not on characters, but on intense transpersonal emotions borne by characters...

SUSAN SONTAG, *Against Interpretation*

Whenever the races blurred they entered the stream of reality.

GHALIB, "XV," trans. Adrienne Rich

I need someone hand, to lead me through the night...

IRMA THOMAS, "I Need Your Love So Bad"

CONTENTS

DIALECTICS OF LIBERATION ACCORDING TO CARLEEN ANDERSON

I think I'm found; I feel unbound.

'On the waste, beneath the sky . . .'

They caught him yesterday night. During the NCAA Tournament game on CBS. He called the Athens Police. Georgia. Said he wanted to turn himself in and that he had 8 hostages and that he wanted to surrender on live television so that if they shot him down trying to surrender everyone would see it. It's pretty clear he shot the two police officers. It's definite that one of them is dead and the other is going to survive the gunshots to his face and shoulder. It's unclear if Ohio State can beat Kentucky, and it's been clear to me for years that advertising sold to sporting events is designed to make men partially numb and to make them despise the parts of themselves that aren't.

In ways related to some or none of this, there's dense weather in my house tonight.

'the one above . . .'

'the other beneath . . .'

When I lived in Alphabet City, Manhattan, in 1990, I used to leave
my car, an early 80s Dodge Omni, unlocked with a sign UNLOCKED!
on the dash. On clear nights, I left the windows down. In the morning
when I went out to switch it to the alternate side of whatever street,
routinely, I'd find some blurry man asleep in the back seat. It's
romance to invest his "this you, man? my bad, my bad. . ." with more
than a sliver of dignity; a sharp smell, like the smell that comes out of
subway vents in the street, left by those men in the seats worked away
from romance in any case.

One clear night in July it stormed suddenly and I woke up and
thought about my car and said fuck it and in the morning I came out
to find that someone rolled up all four windows of my car. That's true.
And then—and the truth is that in my mind it's the same person,
which certainly says more about me than about whoever it actually
was—they threw a brick thru each of the windows of my car. One
brick. Four times. When I came out in the morning it was alone in
the backseat. Car flooded. Me thinking: someone did all this in the
rain? Or maybe it was four people, strangers to me and each other, who
found in my Dodge Omni, somehow, the impulse to perform this one,
intricately repetitive act?

While the car still had its windows, one man had climbed in, rolled
them up, and locked himself inside. I knocked on the glass to no effect

in the morning. He's in there, face down. *Out.* As it's said: dead to the world. I stared to see if his back moved. It did. I had to go back up the street and up the stairs and search for the key to the doors which I hadn't used in months. No key. I call a locksmith.

It strikes me now, reading this, how this page provides a space that didn't then exist in my world. A reader, for instance, may wonder why not call the police? The thought occurs to me now, too. But, it didn't then. But now, too, I can see that my world, then, also had no space for me to write about what was happening in my world. "In me," also, a space I had no space for then. Now something in me looks back and wonders. Is the space of this page in me? And is that the same space as the idea to call the police? I suspect it is and so it's hard for me to trust this page in me, now, that didn't exist then.

Man one still in there, *out.* I'll spare you the scene with the locksmith upon his seeing the out man in my car and me out with no key to get in. $50 to the locksmith. When I unlocked the car, man one, having slept thru the locksmith scene, woke up perfectly lucid and suggested a $5 fee for guarding the car all night.

'that before him...'

Lately, I've taken to sleeping with all the windows in the house wide
open. The noise from the night train, from the air conditioning (in
March?) of the office building across the street, something with claws
verging into hands digs in the leaves the electric chorus of birdshriek
when the neighborhood owl's in the air the sirens going to E.R. the
silent twirl of scent from Reg's insomniac pipe two doors down.
Outside is colder than inside and the invisibly-evident world falls over
the sill onto the cursive capital *K* of Stacey's body under the covers.
The gentle, beautiful, avant-blues when Ed—our reclusive neighbor—
sits on his porch and plays his flute. I gather the rhythms like kindling
and it's true I measure them all against the legal availability, almost
a civic duty, of firearms in Georgia. And, these few nights, now, the
blades of the search helicopters, what Mzée calls, "Ka-Ka-hopters," in
thru the window, falling on and around the bed.

I feel the labor of feeling orbit the room. Gradients of pressure concave
and convex. The obvious, invisible structures of this state where we've
lived six years. Georgia. A bat flies in the window loops the ceiling fan
and flies out. 100 grams of sonar, fur and flight and, for five seconds,
my phobic back glued to the sheet. This state in orbit, a convexity
in which I feel like feeling feels like a conspiracy, a concavity, a silent
volume, *this* state, trying to make a mime of me.

'behind him...'

'On all sides of him . . .'

Jamie Hood. In 2001 his brother was shot dead by Athens police. He has five other brothers. And five sisters. I learn this from Stacey who learns it from the women at work. The Atlanta stations have been showing his photo for days, the background of the photo has darkened since its first appearance and, somehow, the darkening darkness of the backdrop has collected in and around his eyes lending an attendant weight, *menace* I'd guess, to his face and aging him by a decade. Now, after serving 12 years in prison, he's paroled, 33 years old, and on the run for the past three days after shooting two police.

News breaks into the broadcast of the NCAA Tournament and there he comes out the door, no shirt—to *prove* he wasn't armed. His family and some of the family of the hostages, several of whom knew each other, stand down the street and watch together on the monitors of the TV vans. Jamie Hood twitches on camera. His face pulled to the side. I look to see if he's crying but he's not, the twitch an action of his shoulders not his chest.

They didn't shoot Jamie Hood tonight. They cuffed him bare-chest down directly atop a fire ant colony. In back of the TV reporter, three police to the side of the SWAT van frantically brushing one another's collars and arms and backs. Some of the Hood family and some of the hostages' families hold hands and stare at the ground, praying in thanks.

My old sign UNLOCKED! a flash in my eyes.

The reporter: "Police are relieved tonight to have apprehended Hood before the slain officer's funeral on Sunday."

'whichever way he turned...'

Jamie Hood will go back to his place, another place, to another kind of permanent absence from the civic world of Georgia. Worlds. To the largely invisible, overwhelmingly black world of the Georgia prison system and most likely to the electric chair (still in use in GA) or lethal injection chamber in Butts County, where the state will soon murder Troy Davis. If he makes it that far; and the TV splashes blue on the wall and we go back to basketball. And, I sit with Milan wondering, you know, how to raise him and be a person and teach a class and map the weather in the house when something in me was really hoping, insanely, maybe, that Hood would get away. Itself a stupid fantasy, "away?"

We're sentenced to ourselves. I know those sentences mean something to each other. So, the space implied by semicolons at best; or worst. In moments I'm struck to terror at how little I really trust outside this troubled weather in my house. I wonder about that sentence. Windows wide open. Imaginary semicolons turning in the breeze like mobiles. I wonder about style. How we wear it all: the fact of depending on all kinds of things that can't possibly be trusted. And, people aren't things.

      —*'not in the stars, Brutus...'* burnt in the bridge each in the other—

Now, an ad for some light beer where the woman bartender verbally divests some fool of what we're to take (by its absence) to be his

9

(meaning our) manhood. I tell Milan that all advertising debases people who watch it. It has to do that. He nods. How else get people to buy all this shit? He nods. Stares ahead. TV on his face in blue and red flashes. Crime scenes. I watched him watch the rest of whatever game turning around in my head the piece of my being that, no matter what I know, still feels sick at the prospect of state power's abstract reign over the living absurdity and, really, the killing criminality, of this antisocial structure.

'from which it may be inferred...'

If there was a gun to shoot the part of men that laughs at ads like these beer commercials I'd buy the gun. But, there's no gun like that. And, there are no hands to touch thru the caul of numbness that protects whatever withered slice of a person is the real target of this economy. That's success. My culture calls the wither itself a privilege which is part of why the terror which means it's part of why I don't have a culture.

Meanwhile, how many black men have I watched "brought to justice" in images like these of Jamie Hood? It's a never-ending stream of images, in a way, at this point, whether we look or not, a continuous stream back to back to name it . . .

Greg Velasquez. He was a good DJ. Called himself "The Law." That's true. Dropped out of high school in Chicago, Fenger High I think, and moved to Madison, Wisconsin to disappear into the college scene and spin records. And, he did. And we were friends. And, once in a while I'd see Greg wearing glasses he didn't need with a notebook leaving some or other huge lecture class he wasn't registered for, and he brought his little brother with him and put him through high school in Madison while he did what he did and on March 9, 2004, he had a nervous breakdown and went to look for his daughter at Red Caboose Daycare on Williamson Street. She no longer went there. When he insisted that they bring her to him and they refused he came up with a knife, or maybe it was a cleaver, somehow. When the police arrived there was a standoff. The kids huddled in an adjacent room, Greg, broken and incoherent, wielding a blade. The police shot him seven times in the chest with 9MM bullets. The incident was termed SUICIDE BY POLICE.

'the waste also, needless to say . . .'

'was of a dark colour...'

In the Wisconsin State Journal, the local newspaper, the following: "Officer Jean Papalia, standing behind the two shooters, told an investigator when she saw 39-year-old Gregory Velasquez with the knife, 'she knew they were going to have to kill him.' The fusillade of shots sounded like the officers were 'out at the range,' Papalia said."

In 1990, in my living room, asked on film about his work as a DJ Greg said: "You have the woman or the man singing at the top of their lungs when the crowd is at their peak. Then you take out the beat, the crowd throws their hands up and they scream and they just go off... it gets to a point, particularly in house culture, when it's almost a religious experience. I've seen people get to the point where they were crying they were so much in tune to the atmosphere; crying with relief; crying with enjoyment."

SUICIDE BY POLICE Christ, I think, who does *that* happen to?

And I read that days after he was shot a city worker found Greg's journal in a plastic bag in Tenney Park. The first sentence apparently reads, "I wear my heart on my sleeve..." and that sounds like Greg, but that's all I read, because I'd have to subscribe to the data service to read the full article, and, really, having known Greg, I feel like I know the rest anyway which I don't, of course, and I hate *that* feeling of already knowing in myself which is why write—to replace the lie of the already known—and why I'd love to read that journal.

Last time I saw him alive was on CNN coverage of The Million Man March. The camera panned the crowd and paused, for a second, a full close up, on Greg's rapt face listening to the speech as if the sun itself was speaking the words. By the time I thought, "That's Greg!" the camera had panned on.

Stacey and I are married, 14 years and three kids, and we argue, and sometimes our arguments are so obviously about an inarticulate fact that we don't know what to do or why in any way other than the most literal: dishes, laundry. Who's got the baby? Who forgot to flush and left a load in the toilet! And, sometimes I end up accusing her of putting an invisible barrier between herself and the world and I tell her that I think she thinks I'm too exposed to—the terms of which exposure feel to me like a kind of banishment from—the world. And I think I'm right, and that means I think she is too, but that doesn't always mean I have the faintest idea, in my hands, of how to touch her and maybe that makes her feel like I'm part of the world that warrants the invisible barrier.

14 years and Stacey says at least six of them don't count so more like eight than fourteen, and I say those here-and-there years, okay the bad ones, damn-straight count, in fact double, so more like twenty than eight.

And private rituals. Or, if private from the private does that mean secret? I mean if private means secret from the public? As opposed to intimate which must mean simply on terms that don't exist in public. I've known people terrified of each of these spaces, and I've never met anyone fluent across them all. I know a few who are closer, I think, than I am and I know it took them years of pain and play and labor to get there. Real intelligence.

'with certainty . . .'

15

'it seemed a dark absence...'

So, private. And, I remember things and sometimes try to touch myself, and often what I remember doesn't feel like my life and what I touch doesn't really feel like me at all. And, by lyric, I mean somehow invisibly and inaudibly—which isn't exactly to say uncontrollably—fluent, and by lyric I mean to know that, if this is true for me, for us, it's true for many.

'the mirage of union...'

In a "Daybook" of paper stapled together by George Oppen ca. 1964, he wrote:

> There is the area of Lyric—the
> area in which one is absolutely
> convinced that one's emotions
> are an insight into reality
> and death
> But values—as they say—

—a Dominican band plays at a friend's picnic. One summer back when there were only four of us and we sat on a blanket watching the band, Stacey gets up and walks away and a woman sitting with her kids and four—maybe?—sisters turns to me smiling and asks me a question in Spanish. The other women turn to look at me. I say I don't understand. She: your wife, she speaks es-Spaneesh? Me: no, not really. And she: Is she Dominican? And me: no, she's black. The women bounce looks off each other and back to me. Kids oblivious. She: jou mean black black? Me: yes, blackblack—

'the dark colour was so dark . . .'

When it rains everything's wet. When it snows everything's white. Nature doesn't miss. And, my recurring dream that I stand nude down the block from the streetlight in a silent snowfall. Face to the light back to the wind. And, I feel the flakes sap dreamheat where they land on my outstretched arms, the back of my skull. And, I turn around and no snow at all has fallen where my shadow lies, long, from my feet like a body-shaped grave in the bone-colored light of the street. And, I try to lie down in that open space, that space beyond nature, unknown to culture, but the space disappears as I crouch toward it.

'the color could not be . . .'

The civic world of Georgia, oh, now I mean another one. In my class, Black Music in American Writing, in 2011, at the University of Georgia where they've just concluded a month-long celebration 50 YEARS OF DESEGREGATION I play "The Star Spangled Banner" sung by Marvin Gaye at the 1983 NBA All Star Game in Philadelphia. I talk about Marvin singing the nation, at the time, Reagan's nation, back into proximate, viable concert with, to use a brutal phrase, *black life*. A rhythm track and a song-length homonym. Georgia is 40 percent black. There are no black students in this class of 30—50 YEARS—and far as I can tell the students think I beamed down from some fictional planet. Their faces talk to me: "Is he black? Part black? He *can't* be white. Is he? *Can* he?" We talk a little about music and space, public space, private space, social space, intimate space. What type of songs go in what spaces and why? "Even national space," I say, and "Marvin's kind of connected the *national* and the intimate, the private, in his song. Can you hear that?"

Students are nodding. An "anthem." Then I say, obviously, there's the actual black, or 'Negro', national anthem. They look at me silently. I say, "there is, right, you all know there's a black national anthem." The students stare at me in silence. I say, "Lift Every Voice and Sing"? Nothing. I ask how many of the students grew up in Georgia. All but a few raise their hands. And, the state's 40 percent black, and every one of those persons knows this song, the anthem of a kind of nation, and you all have never heard of it? Apartheid. And, I'm thinking, how do I get to this fictional planet these kids (who are not kids!) think I'm from? I wonder for a moment of my *own* silence, and I think, on this planet, there'll be no *information*. I hear sky and waste.

'could not be identified...'

'the usual luminaries were absent . . .'

Samuel Beckett wrote his novel *Watt* in English while hiding from the Gestapo in Roussillon d'Apt in the early 1940s. As a footnote to the addenda of the novel he notes: "The following precious and illuminating material should be carefully studied. Only fatigue and disgust prevented its incorporation."

In the ADDENDA:

> *on the waste, beneath the sky, distinguished by Watt as being, the one above, the other beneath, Watt. That before him, behind him, on all sides of him, there was something else, neither sky nor waste, was not felt by Watt. And it was always their long dark flowing away together toward the mirage of union that lay before him, whichever way he turned. The sky was of a colour, from which it may be inferred that the usual luminaries were absent. They were. The waste also was of a dark colour. Indeed the sky and the waste were of the same dark colour, which is hardly to be wondered at. Watt was also very naturally of the same dark colour. This dark colour was so dark that the color could not be identified with certainty. Sometimes it seemed a dark absence of colour, a dark mixture of all colors, a dark white. But Watt did not like the words dark white, so he continued to call his darkness a dark colour plain and simple, which strictly speaking it was not, seeing that the colour was so dark as to defy identification as such.*

The civic world of Georgia. And, of course, two of the women at Stacey's job know the Hood family. 12 kids, most of them wild. Parents wild, too. One of them said her sister's daughter dated Jamie Hood in high school and he used to call the house til her husband insisted that only he answer the phone. A father in the home. And, I think to myself, I bet he didn't sleep with his windows wide open. A filigreed, locked, steel gate over the front door. One tells a story she knows from the 90s about the Hoods and another family shooting it out across the parking lot of Pinecrest Apartments. Bullet holes in the neighbors' cars. Several of the women know the black officer recovering from gunshots. None of them know the white officer who was killed. They say that the wounded officer went to Timothy Road Baptist, said 'everybody knows him.' They say that's the way it is, it's the good ones that always get shot. Then two other women say, 'everyone knew that black cop was dirty, Hood shot the white one by accident, he had a fight with the other one about who owed who what for months.'

'indeed the sky and the waste...'

'a dark absense of colour...'

Milan will go to Clarke Central High School next year. He says it's
called "Dark Central" by kids at the suburban high school across the
county line that runs just to the south edge of town. Last year the
principal told a group of middle school parents, "this is a city school,
we have all kinds of kids here, I like to tell people we send them to
Yale and we send them to jail." I come home and ask Milan if he thinks
they spell "Darke Central" with an e? And Milan, laughs, "probably."

'a dark mixture of all colours...'

'the waste also...'

And, a few weeks later, I had separate conversations with two women
(one of whom clearly thinks she's 'white' and I'm not sure about
the other one) colleagues who'd come to my office with professional
questions and then, incidentally, wanted to stress (to me?) their
commitment to public schools. This out of the blue. Then each drew
up tears in her eyes and told me of the terrible decision they'd had
to make about switching their children out of Clarke Middle School.
Two in a week. And, "what did I think about Athens Academy?" I
said I didn't really think about Athens Academy, "I know it was the
'white academy' across the county line created in the 70s when they
desegregated the Athens schools and that someone, a dean I think, had
told me it'd been kept afloat largely by UGA professors sending their
kids there." One of the women, openly crying by now, told me that
her son wasn't thriving where he was. She asked me how Milan was
doing and I said I think he's doing fine and I looked at her tears and
felt violence swirling in the space between us—the space filled exactly
with the difference, whatever it is, between what I call "fine" and what
she calls "thriving." I thought to myself, in an electric kind of pain,
"what am I supposed to say about a school, an 'Academy,' formed to
avert, even to foreswear, the so-called 'criminal' consequences of our
mongrel lives." Sentences. And 'Not in the stars...'

'a dark white...'

Thrive, *v*. I. intr. To grow or develop well and vigorously; to flourish, prosper 2. Of a person or community: To prosper, increase in wealth, to be successful or fortunate. b. Of a thing: to be successful, turn out well 1587. Hence: **Thriveless** a. (*poet.*) not thriving, unsuccessful, profitless. **Thriver** (now *rare*), one who or that which thrives.

'which is hardly to be wondered at . . .'

When Milan was in fourth grade we were driving on Finley Street, projects on both sides of the street, and Milan: there go the ghetto . . . And me: what the hell does that mean, man? And he: that means that that's where the mean kids get on the bus. And me thinking he lives here, I don't, and I don't know what to say, so I say into the mirror "Milan, sometimes people seem mean when they're really, really scared." He nods in the rearview mirror. A few years later I'm raging around the house about *$350!* on a Sunday because Milan hadn't quite yet got around yet to mentioning quite yet that his glasses (second pair) had been borrowed off his face on the bus to school on Friday. Monday. There we are with Vice Principal Williams who: what grade are you in, son? And Milan: seventh. And Williams: well, when you going to start acting like it? Silence. And Williams: I've got the glasses. But, I want to know why you didn't report the theft to me. Milan: they weren't stolen. Williams: did you say he could have them? Milan: no. Silence. And, Williams: you didn't report the theft because you want to be *cool*. Don't be a snitch, right? Milan halfnods. Silence. Williams: let me tell you something, that's a criminal mentality and that is *not* your *life*-style.

'the color was so dark . . .'

'…which strictly speaking it was not…'

In the fall of 2013, Italo Calvino's letters were published. In a review of the collection, I came upon the following quotation that shimmered in my eye and made me remember "Verbatim Breaking News: …" I had no recollection of the passage. I went home and found my copy of *Invisible Cities*. There it was, with my underlines, noted with stars, and apparently forgotten. Or maybe it'd been replaced, syllable by syllable in these pages. So, I splice:

> The inferno of the living is not something that will be; if there is one, it is what is already here, the inferno where we live every day, that we form by being together. There are two ways to escape suffering it. The first is easy for many: accept the inferno and become such a part of it that you can no longer see it. The second is risky and demands constant vigilance and study: seek and learn to recognize who and what, in the midst of the inferno, are not inferno, then make them endure, give them space.

'a dark colour plain and simple...'

And, today, I heard on the radio that the Mayor has asked the citizens of Athens to "line the road" leading from the murdered police officer's funeral (held in the biggest indoor theater in town) to the cemetery. Didn't catch the name of the cemetery, I've never been to one in Athens. Who, I wonder, is that show for? It can't be for the slain officer. Who is such a spectacle designed to leave touched? Who untouched? Who untouchable? But, then, who is who, really? And, who is that? And, who isn't? And to whom?

'so dark as to defy identification...'

CRITIQUE OF CONTEMPORARY AMERICAN POETRY

Section 1: the poets
    What's *wrong* with people?

Section 2: the poems
    What's wrong with *people*?

THIRSTLOVE

The place is extent : set on the table;
exact : : raw spool of yarn and a glass of red wine.

A candle burns in the glass burns
an ellipse above the shadow of your head on the wall.

Acclimate, in eye-pulse curette   the light.

You toss the spool and the yarn loops
over a tarnished arm,
the lamp hangs by its neck from the ceiling.

The point is to let the fingers act let act
the mind let watch let thirst for sight.

Dip the frayed end in the glass. Close up.

The liquid climbs the impossible paradigm
of fibre. Watch; when you blink
the center of the earth escapes into space.

Inscape. To blink is the law.

Interruption. A murrey fibre.

Dread the inability, the liquidity, to liquid the law, to love the truth

which is love's only real demand; the paradigm
remains undyed.

The degree of thirst, the
extent : exact : :
love fails to tell the liquid what it lost,
in the climb climb climb from climb none   rappel.

Drop by drop.

That skin made invisible gloss, made inaudible
talc shudder in stations
of thunder.

Please, now. Laugh first laugh your laugh last.

State this absolutely plain: love's truth moves
in a paradigm (we think it's terror
but it's only thirst) which knows
no dread worthy of its respect for liquid's quiddity.

Undistracted
by us, by personal ploys of plane and soft rain of bright curls, knows
the wood is never plumb true or shaved raw
the skin stretched over motion beneath
and gliss-sweat sure but never bare along its open
grain.

Love's thirst for raw wood and
whatever it actually is, perfect metal, that's all
laid all along the all beyond in the name
of skin.

The open grain isn't in (nor of) the wood any more
than sound can live in the uncut
space of a single voice.

The paradigm is practical
isn't in the yarn's fluid or
in the wine's fibre.

At the bus stop in the rain, the man with the pocketful
of names told me : that paradigm
and a nickel get you change for a quarter.

Flake of ash onto
wet concrete : mesenchyme, subsusurrus fascia.

Sibilant, in tongue-touch curette   the sound.

Limbs do twitch, the barrel roll of horizon,
the 20 seconds of consciousness
when air held, somehow, open, slams shut.

What's alive in a life?

Lyric guillotine. Cuts. Cuts close.

The closed (rhymes with toast) crease between the real
wood and any extent : exact : : of skin darker (which is to say always)
than what's truly raw (which is to say never)
or really bare.

A dream of metaphoric rope :
extent : : tied into a real noose : : : exact.

The dream of waking
up stripped to the skin, the wine in fibres : ex
tent : of one eye and, with the other,
you're forced to watch (and fail to see)
salt draw from what surrounds, to draw together : : ex
act : : lost climb of raw skin in the grain, first tremor, a living wood laid bare.

SUMMERTIME OR SOMEWHERE *JUST* (SOUTH OF)
ABOVE MY HEAD

The photo above the fold of *The New York Times*
today, Monday, May 14 is captioned: "Mourners gathered at the home
of Mullah Arsala Rahmani, a member of the High Peace Council
who was killed Sunday. Page A4."

Twenty twelve.

 The strip-patch of mail tape
on the floor to my left glistens in the wet light after the rain,
and I think about the scar in the wood and my mind turns
back to yesterday.

 Sunday.

 We know the truth is never the truth,
but at least it's a place to start.

 Again & again
to start and you never really know—
because of how often things sound
one way and feel like something else
and also at the same time because you know
if you wink both eyes at once it's not two
winks it's one blink
—whether you can feel yourself wink your life
or ever hear yourself blink apart.

Again and here we are in this house built in the South
and these roles dice-cast, glass-blown
inside historical iron.

I but blink & you slash at my eye
with your voice.

Your face made of again & somewhere
else.

In the next room a woman
Basie called William sings "This Year's Kisses"
and she drops "above" on the ground
& rubs out the coal's red eye with her heel.

Tone in her voice staring above down
for all it ever claimed to be and you steady at me
and "Without Your Love" fills the room next and she hits
that "above" and she does it again.

Above down
on the ground, again & again,
and I hear Prez float somewhere softer than low
and it all feels like slippery flame
in my dish-soap hands and I remember
Bill Matthews said what Lester Young
did was like the melody dreaming about itself.

And I can feel myself thinking I know touch
is never the touch but where the hell else
and Monk telling Coltrane here's a minor chord
with the third out and Trane
well then how do you know it's a minor
chord if the third's out
and Monk because the third I left out
is flat and I remember Reinaldo Arenas wrote in jail
everything is obvious
and then it appears to me that these houses
that breathe so you can smell shifts of dark
in the night air outside let's face it
weren't built for us and what gives
in the floor ain't nothing but thin planks of pine
and something too small to see
eating at them from beneath and I see it
come over us again like again's invisible skin
again & again you know
like it does until it's the thing to swipe the dishes
clean from the Formica and put a little oak
side chair thru the dining room floor
and it opens like a mouth a bright surprise in long worn weather.
    It's violence, yes, up on down
wood on wood.

    Oak on pine.

And, that invisible Southern stuff
they tell us on the news is the air,
not to say the stuff they tell us on the air is the news,
breaks open too and there we are, again, and so now
what?

Halved by the fold in the *Times*, a photo of a man
who saws at a tree limb.

It's a story about a woman
crushed by an elm while sitting in Stuyvesant Square
Park.

She lived.

At a glance, the story says
that when "panicked parkgo-
ers" tried to get the 30-foot limb off she screamed
"I don't want to die."

It's news today. Monday.
All this happened
yesterday and I hear myself, yesterday, say "I know hell is anyplace
that can't be described" and you nod at the fresh slash
in the floor and touch my shoulder and all that hell that slash
gone, again, from your voice.

And you know gone again means here again.

And again, we think it means time
but we won't deal with this in time because this time
isn't made of time it's made of us and so
we'll deal with this in us.

So again means us.

In the crawlspace
underneath the house the damp heat coming out
of the earth feels cold on my back and with my hands
I can feel another song,
"Long Gone Blues," begin
thru the rough-hewn underside of the floor.

I push up from beneath and you push down from above
and smooth out the fresh slivers
with quick strips of thick, clear tape.

Under this dry rain,
bits of wood and dust, I hear the roll rasp and slice
and think, once even this long gone song was new
and I know that's not true
but I hear Tab Smith stretch an alto
out over the break like two handfuls of hot taffy
and twirl Gershwin
backward and I think I can almost make out what

Hot Lips Page growls mute, out of that now
which was his and I think about the they're-all-dead now
of this now and when *that* when was now
our parents were hardly even born.

On the one-year anniversary
of Osama bin Laden's killing, President Obama flew
in secret to Kabul to address, well, to address who I wonder?

I know he wasn't talking to me and then, like playing with mirrors,
he was gone before anyone knew he was there.

I said all this happened yesterday but that's not exactly true.

I read the tree-limb piece and found what actually happened
yesterday was that New York City paid the woman $4 million
to settle a suit about its upkeep of the trees
in Stuyvesant Square Park and I think I wonder
if she'll live thru that?

I wonder if I think
her first thought with the news was "I don't want to die."

Under the crushed crushing voice
of the woman called William who called Basie Bill back
Jimmy McLin strums the time into a life
more felt than heard and I feel that in the floor above
my head and I figure that's what he's there to do

which is a lot and we're going to vote for Obama
damned straight, because we think it's true that the power
killing us will kill us slower with him there than if he wasn't, that's
     about it.

     That and he's got some style, too, give him that what the hell.

     And, too, knowing
what all we know he knows, if we watch with vision densed down and
so slower than the speed of light, the velocity of media, we'll gain traces
     of the actual—as opposed to elliptical—shape of that office.

     Even a stealth moment in the shadow of who owns it, which means what
     owns us . . .

     . . . some blue grid of ice in that which what owns *in* us owes—

     And, yesterday, my back on the cold heat of the damp
earth, I can feel it now, how I thought I could see
hell very clearly from under there and there
seemed like a whole lot of there out there
and the kids either we raise them up or they're pulling us
down or maybe both but before we're done
there they go with they own
brains out into it
and, from that there, I could see that maybe that what love means
is this house and this old, newly busted up floor,
in this new South, in this old now

for us, for who knows how many, now, articulate,
where all hell defined above be damned below
and love is a place where nothing can touch us
and we don't have any choice
but that, and by that I mean hell defined above, and here below
that'll *be* that—as in when it all be's
like that—if—and I hear Mzée's steps above my head
his three-year-old voice chants "beez
in the trap be-beez in the trap"
and he's right—so that'll be
that trap if we don't find a way of touching it back

BECAUSE TRANE WOULD HAVE BEEN 87 TODAY: SEPTEMBER 23, 2013

We tried to outpace the thing that chased us, that said: 'You are nothing.'
 — JESMYN WARD

I.

photos shoot what can't be
shot extrusion of what :
what still can still never still hoof-flash wing-blink
hands down in ear-pause we watch
the eye attack itself faced with evidence
which is the lack of vision faced with the photo as if what
all the eye does is choose
the visible from the invisible extrusions of :
a girl from Marrakesh leans off the Tower of Homage
at Gibraltar susurrus her summon her simoom
Calyx of Held a fugitive erotics
of vesicle & cleft Santiago Ramón y
 Cajal his carriage at the drawbridge his eyes
scan a torrent of arm mistress rhythms of the Besòs
in a pale hand covered by a shawl

TRANE: If one of my friends is ill, I'd like to play a certain song and he'll be cured.

43

—float the spring of 1957—

the supple shadow of shade   a streetlight spot streaked diagonal
by a telephone pole at Cooper Square
Juanita Naima stands outside the 5 Spot Café   listens
to Nellie Monk borrow a cigarette from Orrin Keepnews
Nica lights it with a flame-thrower

she kept in her purse   during a break between sets Keepnews asks
Trane   again   about his contract   Trane : I signed with Prestige three
weeks ago   mid-March   Nellie : why
set the flame so high?   and Nica : so I can smoke in the rain

II.

this blare of light is cleft enough
is an open page   a signature of evaporated scars
Headline in Fiction : February 22 1967 : 'Coltrane
and Rashied Ali Survive
Termination Shock, Traverse the Heliopause': *Interstellar Space*

It was because I love you that I said exactly what I said
the paragraph this poem demands can
only surrender or injure   or injure   extrusion of what
a photo can graph   a shovel severs
the root one sought to replant   transplant   the pause in a photo
where one ear touches an untouchable

hand   Calyx of Held   echolocation   September 21 2013   two years to the day
after his state murder in Georgia   people hold hands
in the DeKalb County Library   chant : 'I Am Troy Davis'

———————————————————————————————

TRANE : When he'd be broke, I'd bring out a different song, and
immediately he'd have all the money he needed.

—float the spring of 1957—

lyric time is time made of other times   a missing
photo of what's missed
in a photo   it's important to know leap & gap   Bronislaw
Kaper met Shoenberg in Los Angeles   he said
'people call me Edward Kane'
in 1941 Kaper's Kane wrote "While My Lady Sleeps" for a musical
titled *The Chocolate Soldier* starring a Philadelphia iron worker
turned opera star named Nelson Eddy

III.

Last Friday   John said   [and this isn't Coltrane but the black man
with a bike and a can of beer in a bag sitting on the city's steps across
from the house]   he said   after I finish this   I ain't going to lie
I'm going back in for a year   maybe
two   probation officer said if I don't have work   don't have a job
I'm going back in for a year   maybe
two   I ain't bothering nobody   ain't fucking with nobody   I ain't going to lie

Voyager 1 interstellar probe was launched September 5 1977   it exited
the Heliopause in August 2012   engineers can't determine
the precise date

On Thursday July 10 2013   21-year-old Marshan Bradley was charged
with aggravated battery for shooting 7-year-old Christian Lyles
in Nat Cole Park   Chicago   on the 4th of July   one of 70-some shootings
in the city over the holiday weekend

TRANE: But what these pieces are, and what is the road to attain the
knowledge of them, that I don't know.

—float the spring of 1957—

call it stubborn call it a photographic ostinato   a lyric leap
from Eddy's troubadour serenade
of Risë Stevens   sound engineer Rudy
Van Gelder can't determine   sotto voce
if Paul Chambers is the leap or the bridge   the gap is take
one taped over via Weinstock method   Gitler called it 'a final eerie note'

lyric time   a missing
photo of what's missed
in a photo   Coltrane / Prestige 7105   photo of a horn taken on a horn

IV.

I looked for work now   dishwasher   shit like that   I even went down
over there   you know   to that Mexican place   Agua Linda?
yeah   said: 'might you all need   you know   a dishwasher?'

John squints his eyes and smiles : 'ah   no   I'm sorry we don't have anything'
eyes back   when you and I know what she was really thinking: nigger
you know we keep it in the family—

The Calyx of Held   among the largest in the body   the torrent
of Besòs beyond
the bridge of rhythm in a wrist   the shawl beyond the place of place

according to Reuters   one of the men in Chicago who shot 13 people by
spraying bullets into Cornell Park on September 19 2013 said   we
'were not aiming at anybody'

at the Termination Shock the solar wind falls
below the speed of sound   engineers can't precisely locate what happens
in the hands from what happens to the hands

_____

TRANE: The true powers of music are still unknown.

49

—float the spring of 1957—

May 31   his first recording date as a band leader
Trane made the leader's minimum   union scale at double time
said it made him feel like
playing two notes at once   a chromatic chord on a horn
Gus Khan in one ear
Mal Waldron on Billie's borrowed time to the left
Johnny Splawn at his side   and Trane pulls that last '. . . Sleeps' apart
his first polyphonic
note on record   futility is a C-minor 11TH   a solid B-flat coming out
one side of your mouth   and   with the other
an F up an octave   you blow Nellie
and Nica's smoke away from your wife's face

V.

when an allergy affects the eye the eye attacks the eye

as in a photo which disappears everything

not visible   as in an eye that sees

a park full of nothing   full of nobody

to aim at   meanwhile   the song must be something

like how the ear

slips out the photo's side door   [cut to photo] : the side door

John : maybe two   I ain't bothering nobody

[and waving up at where I live]

ain't up in them people's houses

I ain't gonna lie   the first one was my fault   okay   over there

around the back of Weaver D's   public

indecency   she said she wanted to get high

I ain't messing with nobody

In Artie Shapiro's living room   August 22 1955

Billie Holiday hums

'Please Don't Talk About Me When I'm Gone'

off mic: 'the fuck key I do it in?'

[Jimmy Rowles   the piano player   laughing]

Now it's 1967 : Coltrane's shoes could use

a polish   he's got a pain in his side

I'm a few months old   "5:30 AM"   a poet a friend of mine

confides she's got a fox gone to earth in her chest

I admit   these days it's been hard to precisely

locate a good reason for reason

I smell sunshine & blue smoke comes out of my mouth

my eye hunts

itself and for what slips in and out of ears for what

sounds when friends fall between sounds   if an

analogy affects an enemy   then let's let

inferno the enemy inferno the enemy

TRANE: To be able to control them must be, I believe, the goal of every

musician.

RENDITION OF A PYRRHONIST

—after Friedrich Hölderlin's "Die Titanen"

I.

but not is it though
    Time
if breath that prayer of un-demand
    of transit if to stand as to   adumbrate

to jad to   down to   empale
Eric Holder in Gonzales's chair on John Yoo's lap /
    Hölderlin in Autenrieth's mask

but   not is it   though
    Time
if en-fluid that walk-dark lake
    of echo if to speak as   to paraphrast

to inviolate to   ijaz as   to abjure   to Guantanamo

[sound: Movement colliding]

II.

but not is it   though
    Time
if seven cylinders of hunger
    of ten-penny moment   blare of nail

but not   is it   though
    Time
if eleven torn spheres of taste
    Samir Khan at a corner table in The Blue Room
Mwembe Tayari   Mombasa   a pair

of smoke-tinted Chevy Tahoes idle
    double parked at the corner
of Turkana and Selassie

of Khan reading *The Star* while a cell phone
    vibrates on the Formica   in the mirror six thick men
in khakis and white polos drag a feather
    merchant into the street

Khan's Nokia : MISSED CALL : NAT WEBB (S. L.)

[sound: Arrow blows past the ear]

III.

but not   is it   though
    Time
if the slim boy with the gun in hand
    of ARMY STRONG   to aim as   to nail into
an azure sky

but not is it though
    Time
if pulsed in the skull   a bright spike of fear
    of Salt Pit denied as   to Aafia Siddiqui

a shadow cast of a ghost prisoner in Kabul
    on the tarmac at Szymany as   to breath in black

site in doggo in space

    [sound: Moment collapsing]

IV.

Pod Alpha [sound: silence : : figure A: nude : hands and feet tied to a chair
in the dark : windowless room : 30 degrees Fahrenheit:
head duct taped to chair back: beats by dre ear buds taped
into ears: 1000 watt flood bulb at the tip of the nose] :   [switch on]

    [chorus in ear buds] :   [translate this page]

to push to pull against pulling to
      pull to push against pushing
to think to real against reeling to

end to fend against rending
to real to reel against thinking to
      rend to end against fending

to gist to jest against blinking to
      fend to rend against ending
to blink to jest against gisting to

  :   [switch off]   :

v.

but   not is it though
    Time
if the well-worn shoe of the perfect
    of all unmade of turned in turn in   turned

Nicht ist es aber / Die Zeit
    if hung upside
down if deaf to nail of light   of hypo-
    thermic needle of all that

unmade exact   in the shape of thirst

    [sound: Moment colliding :   Movement collapsing]

IV.

butnotisitthoughtime butnotisitthoughtime
    if one is in place but one's place is not though
in its place   nonotisitthough nonotisitthough
    at rest if one is in one's moment and such moment
exists but one has no moment in the place
    of one's place if one's place is not
though in its place   notisitindeedthough notisitindeedthough
    one's place if the moment one has in place
is not of the moment of one's moment

one is then evidence as   to not exist   one is then
    moment of another moment   one part
of one grain part as   to infinite arrow of place
    part motion outside the moment of place in place
outside the moment of motion as   to scream
    as   to thwart all mask   to Mask as   to origins in place
not in its place   in motion of all moment
    in sound that
    inaudible arrow / arrow inaudible
outside as   to displaced place and unmoveable moment
    of those who as   to put to
crush   and thereby Arrow of not is it though
    Moment   of Time of not is it   Movement   though

VII.

Pod Zeta [sound : Rozz Williams sings "Forever Came Today"
in continuous loop : : figure B: nude: hands and feet tied
to a chair in a windowless room: 44 degrees Celsius: head duct
taped to chair back: beats by dre ear buds taped into
ears: room lit on ceiling and three walls by 100 1000 watt bulbs :
fourth wall and floor one-way mirrors] :

[sound / light : switch off]

[switch on : chorus of voices in ear buds]   :   [translate this page]

to jest to blink against gisting to
     resist to persist against insisting to
abjure to ensure against enduring

     to insist to resist against persisting
to affix to admix against suffixing to
     ensure to endure against abjuring

to suffix to affix against admixing to
     persist to insist against resisting to
endure to abjure against ensuring

     to admix to suffix against affixing to

{switch off: chorus} : {sound / light: switch on}

VIII.

[aka. Natalie Webb]

the white widow in a sheer black buibui
        smokes a crooked joint   lies
in a hammock of sisal strung across the veranda
        of an abandoned mansion in Nyali

        intelligence collated in Addis
reports her headed south by tuk-tuk at Namanga

        she stares at a wall of bad stucco and sees
a zigzag route to Kiwayu then Kismayo via Watamu via
        Malindi   from San Diego an agent

flies a cormorant shaped stealth drone

in endless serpentine   arabesque
        over resorts in Diani where
village girls hang hijabs in agave sisalana

        and wander in bikinis up the beach   false-lashed
almonds razor in   on khat cut with Juicy Fruit   hover over
        bleach-eyed Australians and red-faced K.C.s, ex-pats v. tourists
pounding their volleyballs into yesterday

        [sound: a shadow dives into the surf beyond the reef]

IX.

but not is it though / the place
    of no moment   not is it though / the arrow

    of no movement   is it though from Abu
Ghraib and hidden by (Army / CIA) fiat
    from the Red Cross / Médecins Sans Frontières
it though published and Pulitzer'd by Dana Priest

    and hidden in the open by fear in a public
with no private   phantasma of the phantom public
    with no place in its arrow of place   committed
to futility as   to commit an act of reason   with

    no movement   is it though   in its mask of the moment

    ]   ::   [

VERBATIM PALESTINE: JUNE 3, 2014

Palestine is a land planted by eyes
refusing to be closed
        —From "JEBU," ETEL ADNAN, 1981

There are places, spectrums of experience, human geographies, invisible to the human eye; you see them with your life. Failing that, you fall blind. In both cases, with an invisible, physical velocity, these places become every place which becomes the nature of—a threshold for—human sight.

West Bank. Occupied Territory. You've seen all this before. You've never seen anything like this. The result is a chart of echoes, irregular. And barriers. Ricochets of a hard rubber ball pitched down the empty length of Shuhada Street in Al-Khalil. In Hebron. Follow the ball. At an empty intersection, no, at an *emptied* intersection, you'll be asked to show ID. If you've got West Bank identification, Israeli soldiers will prevent you from following the ball. You, then, a ricochet; the ball's path a chart of echoes, one moment of a future you never had. An event in a world that happened without you. Picture a world occupied by those ricochets and the echoes they cause. Mid-day. A thin skin of black plastic bags stretched across a cross of sticks rises into a hail of golden, high-elevation Levantine light. A kite floats up out of a parking lot and draws its twine over Al Haram Al Ibrahimi, the Tomb of the Patriarchs. Arms in moments of a compass, oblique, two boys argue the kite's exact position over the neighborhood and the route around what checkpoints it'd take for one of them to stand beneath it. The kite's shadow floats back and forth across the khaki shoulders of two young soldiers stationed at the Christian / Muslim entrance to the mosque-side of the historic site.

It's a peculiarly human death, borne in the particulars of one's interaction with power and in the nature of that power. This death often masquerades as success, or privilege—which is to say as metaphor. By that death, or ricochet, you no longer see the world with your life. Left to their own—which is to say stripped to the level of desire, of performance—deaths such as this pull all relations into their fissured and conical prisms where life narrows into eye and that eye, grown dense by evacuation, into a piece of post-human glass, a lens of the motivating ideology. Ideology, like any amoral political power, falsely assumes the authority of the ground, you its metaphor surrounded by metaphors, among which: riot gear, steel bars, guard towers, surveillance cameras, rubber-coated bullets, tear gas. It's in this way that the *terms* of privilege, of success, of experience—to the extent you believe those metaphors operate on your behalf—vaunt into position, appear by *trompe l'œil* to eclipse the facts of life. One result: people forced to see with their eyes. It's in this way, from our relationship to power, and from the nature of that power, that we assign a level of reality to metaphor.

All these words are yours. They echo and ricochet from your visit
to Al-Khalil / Hebron on June 3rd, 2014 as part of the Palestinian
Festival of Literature. The words are yours; they touch and swing.
They swing past what they touch. They follow a fly up the street away
from the mosque. They split into syllables to pass through the steel
mesh and metal detectors; rejoin into phrases that move between
the children at play with buckets at the water pump behind the
cage enclosing the end of their street. A sentence that looks like the
intricate shadow of razor wire coiled across the back of a child at play.
Words leave dust behind like when you touch a moth's wings; a fly
with a winged word's worth of dust in one-sixtieth of its eye. What
happens to a word's worth when there's no recollection of tranquility?
An invisible rapidity disguised as a paragraph; the sky-stained skin
of tiny, tiny wings. Words. Translucent boys at play with an acid of
echoes and ricochets mocked in the rational path of their bright black
kite on the wind. Thales returns to Miletus with his twin triangles
capable of measuring ships at a distance over water. In effect, the
possibility of travel by sight. And shadow. The straight line the
mirage—if not the Sphinx—of the rational.

You see with your life but, of course, you never see *your* life. Only another human life, a living eye, can see all that. All human sight, then, is a dance in the distance, speaking of metaphors, between lives watched and those watching. Call it whatever one wishes to call it, the vehicle that travels that span is imagined. As is the span, imagined.

Can you imagine living in the prison of your life stripped down to pieces that can be determined as facts? Determined by the lens of an occupying ideology, an ideology motivated to occupy your life by fact?

No. Such a prison can't be imagined which is how such a prison remains prison, by the ideological power of a factual irreality.

Vacuum blue. The sky looks empty enough to drink the black speck of kite and swallow the boys that hold it by its hypotenuse twine. Two settlers, a man and possibly his teenage son, drive past in a dented, blue Toyota Corolla. The rear of the car almost drags on the street. They leave the vacant, no *vacated*, road behind. Their smiles, the grimmest smiles you can remember, hang like a mobile in the emptied space of the intersection. 'Echoes of what?' you hear yourself wonder. Ricochets. Their eyes carry heavy buckets, a metallic sheen rotates behind their faces; you imagine their vision, wire-brushed and broken by whatever it bounces off, comes back together like if you drop a penny into a wide pool of mercury in a clear glass bowl. Sight by the eyes, blindness by lives evacuated of the senses, bodies haunted by numbness. What happens to a word's worth when someone fills, as someone does, the space in that blue Toyota Corolla and calls that love? In their trunk, twelve stones from a vacated building in the old city: part of a border wall for their garden in Giva't Kharseena. Someone has always called the space of that garden tranquil.

In a letter from "Israel" written on October 8, 1961, the not quite yet famous American writer James Baldwin told his agent, Bob Mills: "I personally cannot help being saddened by the creation, at this late date, of yet another nation—it seems to me that we need fewer nations, not more: the blood that has been spilled for various flags makes me ill... Or perhaps I would not feel this way if I were not painfully—most painfully—ambivalent concerning the status of the Arabs here. I cannot blame them for feeling dispossessed; and in a literal way, they have been. Furthermore, the Jews, who are surrounded by forty million hostile Muslims, are forced to control the very movements of Arabs within the state of Israel. One cannot blame the Jews for this necessity; one cannot blame the Arabs for resenting it. I would—indeed, in my own situation in America, I do, and it has cost me—costs me—a great and continuing effort not to hate the people who are responsible for the societal effort to limit and diminish me."

On June 14, 2014, on a plane, Robert, a retired doctor from Winston-Salem, North Carolina will ask "where have *you* been?" In the conversation that follows you'll realize, again, how one's vision of home, of life, impels one's vision of everywhere else. You'll briefly describe the "wall," the "checkpoints," the division of Palestinian sovereignty into cages within cages depending on the (most often illegal) whim of an occupying power, one's right to movement, among other rights, converted into privilege conveyed by the color of one's ID card. Slipping his folded copy of *Time* magazine into the seat pocket, Robert will say, "Well, Israel has a right to secure its territory." You'll feel an ache in your hands; you realize that almost every word he said needs redefinition. Ricochets. Will imagine this doctor's territory in North Carolina, the life with which he's listening to you: swerving streets and sloping lawns. Secure. Will remember yourself, age 20, with Riccardo Williams and Eric Lassiter, handcuffed to an iron railing and questioned on the Northside of Chicago—North Central Park Ave and Irving Park Road—for sitting on the porch in mixed racial company. Will know you can't tell him that much less this. At the time, early days in the final quintile of the 20th century, you'd never heard a word for "mixed racial company." You all knew you all were cuffed because you were black—you knew, at times, it made no difference that your parents weren't. One chrome thing cuffing your wrist to Ric's, another cuffing your other to Jock Barr's porch railing. Metaphors. Echoes. In row 56 of an aging 747, far enough back so that turbulence doesn't jolt up and down but swings back and forth like a fish tail, will attempt—and fail—to speak to Robert about Palestine from a life in a city of racial checkpoints. It was the same on the South Side, a grid of detainments, false questionings, and harassment. Since

2011, the commander in charge of that regime is in prison—*Time* might have mentioned it. When we were young, all we knew was that it was the law. And *Time* can only ricochet—has no metaphor for—that. You'll remember that Lorca said that, at times, the *duende* is supplied by the listener. Will remember three years ago, age 44, the principal of Clarke Central High School in Athens, GA, where your son, Milan, will go to school the next year, saying "This is a city school, we've got all kinds of kids. I like to say, 'we send them to Yale and we send them to jail.'" Will realize that it's not possible to tell this retired doctor, on his way back from a vacation hiking in Italy, much at all about Al Khalil / Hebron given what he knows and doesn't know—will admit and won't admit about the life he listens with. His ricochets and your echoes. On the plane our bodies contain a level of energy, of power, none could survive for ten seconds; we breathe a metaphor—one too dry to breathe for too long—for air.

June 4th in Akka. In Israel Acre. You wait for a cab to take you to the Sheikh Hussein border crossing, just south of Lake Tiberias, the Sea of Gallilee, where you'll cross into Jordan (in Arabic Buhairet Tabariyya). You walk the streets in what looks like a beach vacation town. You see eyes exiled from the lives they need to see with. Call it whatever you will, it's not a vacation. Metaphor. The shadow of something invisible twirls in a tailspin between you and whatever—which is to say whomever—you see seeing you. Ricochet. You write in a pad: "To be complicit in the orchestration of oppression causes one to relinquish one's hold on experience. Insidiously and by degrees, or by the violence of decision—which is to say conversion—in pursuit of something, the shadow of something, that mostly calls itself safety, or at least stillness, one forfeits the capacity to trust life." Tranquility? Now, you think, "absent that trust one's vision is forced into the eyes, quarantined, and the eyes go to glass, ground into focus by the optics of whatever ideology. Images fixed by whatever camera. Whatever theater of ricochet. Whatever audience for echoes."

You're on Shuhada Street, in Al-Khalil/Hebron. It's June 3rd, 2014. Two boys walk past with a kite and a roll of twine, they're laughing and holding each other by the shoulder. You wonder if it's romance to believe—which is exactly to say, to remember—that they touch each other with their lives, not their hands. The boys turn up into the narrow streets of the neighborhood a few blocks before the checkpoint. A wrist echoes in your eye, it's handcuffed to a porch railing. In a few days, on Saturday, your son Milan, now a Senior at Clarke Central High School, will e-mail to say that the kid he sat next to in U.S. Government, Jordorian Randolph, they called him Jojo, was shot dead in a drive-by shooting on his way home Friday night in Athens. Motive: turf. Whispers: BMF. Suspects: none. He writes to say that no one—which means someone—knows who did it. You type this wondering what to call the space inside that one, slow-moving car on Friday night. You think: "shuttles in the rocking loom of history."

In *Of Cities and Women*, Etel Adnan writes: "I tell myself we are terrorists, not terrorists in the political and ordinary sense of the word, but because we carry inside of our bodies—like explosives—all the deep troubles that befall our countries . . . and traveling doesn't change anything in any way. We are the scribes of a scattered self, loving fragments, as if the parts of the self were writing down the bits and ends of a perception never complete."

It's a chart of echoes, irregular. And barriers. We're scattered in ricochets. You feel the geography of checkpoints and secured territory move through your veins. West Bank. Wherever your eyes land, you feel a pulse from your own territory, your sense of experience, and how it moved from the past through something called you toward whatever else, a future. You see with your life across a span of imagined space. You've seen all of this before. You've never seen anything like this. Cages inside of cages. Cages of belief, of law, of wire and concrete. Machine guns in slings, men in baggy pants saunter like armed men everywhere. Velcro rasp on a bicep. Oily light bent across the lenses of those fucking Oakley sunglasses. Black plastic bags—proto kites— caught on a tangle of rebar. You scan the scene with your life, it looks like a huge flying prison—you won't say concentration—camp crashed here. Half toppled, half upright, part in use, part surplus or refuse, pieces of the wreckage strewn across the scene. Scraps of concrete wall litter a field at angles to what you can't tell. A fire burns at the barrier wall just off the Qalandia Checkpoint, Jerusalem, a mural of Arafat and the imprisoned leader Marwan Barghouti flanked by a guard tower blackened by the flame.

You find that you've been taking a subconscious inventory of the crashed prison camp: cement barriers; the lackadaisical saunter of guards; towers with empty eyes or mirrored windows; razor wire assigned in spirals; other spools tumbleweed'd into wayward stations; discourse of passes and privileges. Something's missing. Then in Akka a clarification. The group assembled to hear from, speak with BDS founder, Omar Barghouti in the open café area of the walled city. Umbrellas and chairs arranged for 20-some. Mid-talk, waves of white smoke begin to curl over the walls in the sea breeze. Waves thicken. Alarms in the cafés sound off. Our eyes run, some pull shirt collars up over their noses and we finish the conversation. Later we learn the fire had been deliberately set, grass on the outside of the walls was burned. Amid questions of timing, you climbed the walls and saw the sloping patches of scorched grass. While Omar discusses and clarifies—"It's a rights movement . . . When it comes to tactics, it's never take it or leave it . . . all considerations are practical, these are not theoretical questions . . ."—smoke thickens obscuring the cafés across the emptied square, fire-flight impulses raise you up in your chair a few times. Something comes alert in your hamstrings. Like the dark center of an open eye in increasing light, the scene's radius closes down around us. A gradual curtain obscures the distance, blurs the blond stones in the crusade-era walls. In hair on your forearm, first, then next to you on Michaels' shoulder, and just to your right in Ahdaf's hair: tiny notes swivel in the air and land. Caught on us, close up, flakes of ash move like gills in faint breaths, in smoke-filled wind.

In a very beautiful essay called "The Light of the South West," Roland Barthes wrote: "I enter these regions of reality in my own way, that is, with my body; and my body is my childhood, as history created it." You know that no seen—which is to say imagined, which means living—territory can ever be secure; it falls endlessly through the people who encounter it. It spins as it falls, the path of that plunging territory is the fluid, fluted core of one's identity. In part, it's the violence of nations to still that spinning. How often by power applied at the border. Citizens, always imagined by each other, might hope, and work, to pilot such a human motion, a living spiral. Motion across—in defiance of—borders. Gravity is a constant. Momentum equals mass times velocity. You've done the math. You've seen all this before. You've never seen anything like this. Borders on the map of one's body.

You've been thinking to yourself that it all feels very American. What you see here looks like the other side of all the one-sided coins flipped all day every day in the U.S. The finely scripted, unspoken sentences, the cultivated and rewarded life-blindnesses of American culture, here, stand for a reality sculpted in concrete and reinforced with legal and military force. You're not the only one who makes the connection; but you're the only one in the group who lives in the American South. Omar Barghouti mentions the Montgomery Boycott; someone in Aida Refugee camp sang "We Shall Overcome." A young man in a Polo shirt with NEGRO printed under his right shoulder sells you the *2013 Legal Unit Annual Report* from the Czech-run Hebron Rehabilitation Committee. The report tabulates violations of Palestinian human rights in Al-Khalil / Hebron by Israeli occupation forces and settlers. Amid tables and photos and pie charts: in 2013 "340 violations... against citizens of the Old Town..." All week you've been sitting in on a conversation between your eyes and your life, you've been arguing with the nature of sight, the limits of lenses. Something taps the crown of a ride cymbal. All week Yusef's poem, "Untitled Blues," in your life's ear. It's an argument with a photo by Yevgeni Yevtushenko of a black boy, a street performer in New Orleans, the poem ends not unlike your week in the West Bank:

> ... The boy
> locked inside your camera,
> perhaps he's lucky—
> he knows how to steal
> laughs in a place
> where your skin
> is your passport.

In a kind of archeological reading, revision, I read and re-read this script of transit. At whatever depth a friend's line unearthed, a couplet in a ghazal, from 7/14/1968:

> Did you think I was talking about my life?
> I was trying to drive a tradition up against the wall.

At the Sheikh Hussein crossing, at the border with Jordan, you flash your blue skin with golden, italic script: United States of America. Pay fees. At the Israeli side you affirm you carry no weapons. In a box-like trailer, you wait for the bus across the river. On the wall a tourism poster of a white family on a beach, a couple and two kids, the little boy holds an American football. No. I check the photo in my phone. It's the father with the football. At the bottom of the poster: *ISRAEL: Where it's vacation time all year round.* At the other end of the trailer, three Arab men sit; they all talk to each other while each sustains another conversation on his cell phone. One breaks off from the talk, flips his phone closed and tries a door at the end of the room. It's locked. His back to you, then, he kneels to pray. Over the shoulder of the man praying hangs another poster. A white woman, blond, in a white bathing suit, floats like a buoy on her back. At the bottom: *THE DEAD SEA: Where time stands still.* At the Jordanian side, you affirm that you carry no bibles. Pay fees. You exit the border in the searing desert sun. I walk slowly. I love the sensation of falling—or is it flying—that comes from walking in the sun across asphalt that pulses and wavers in the heat. I fall or fly across the parking lot to the oasis where the taxi office stands amid the moonscape. More fees. A cab driver installs me in the back of his Camry and rockets us south along the border toward Amman. He turns left up toward the mountains and we climb a flung ribbon of switchbacks through a galaxy of echoes and ricochets.

WITH WORM FOR WORM THE BIRD:
A COSMOLOGICAL FILIBUSTER

but you wouldn't even think it it being
a matter so small said the
bone-colored boy out
the red window of the satin
in the dream that's to
tell me how you learned to walk
without to talk or to talk
without to walk or walk without
to walk or talk without
talk that to say how learned
to taste how comme cosmophagiste
to fall from the mirror of the mirror
into the into of the into
that to say the fall without
the all that to say out the treble in
all the clef-ing
if not all the mother in
the f-ing of the two
not to name a few that
to say of you wouldn't say it it being
a matter of trouble
shared without being
a matter of trouble doubled within
that to say of the sanguine that
not to say of cheer but
chalk of rust of color of old blood
the color of without
what's come from within

color as seen
splashed on country
road windshields
and city street sidewalks
a texture even more than a color
well suited to portraits
that to say renditions
of volume into two dimensions
that to say of collapse
say it inspissation
as in sauté as in sizzling reduction
or radical redaction
such as that that says of life
into speech since speech
a life since life nil said that to say
since life a speech since
speech nil lived that to say that
the majority always
bored here always will
say that to say think
and so from without within they think
at times from within without say
they're the only ones
bored the only ones here
you know all of this by now
that at times without time
we talk so as not to
remember we forget

so as to agree but
you wouldn't say think that that
being a matter
of no relevance that
to say of a fortune well bet
on dice hellbent on fate
that to say on balance on chance
you don't want to read
all that would rather hear
it that's to say I don't want to write
it would rather say
all that all that being the fall without
the all and within
that that thing people say about
a matter of thread
spooled unspooled respooled
you wouldn't hear this this
being merely a matter
of so acute an expulsion
that to say so precise
an anti-climax and you a soot arc
left by the round worn heel of chance
or heel worn round by chance
that to say a dance so don't
I mean don't on the ground
without the ground I mean
the ground you're standing on
without without standing on within

so don't that to say go ahead
we both need the lid
that to say need the lid
closed you to close
out the all and grafted air
to seal in what's best sealed
in and okay okay let's say
lithos sarkophagos
and let's say the mirror-lined
and star-strewn career
of Nut's timeless plunge
that to say flesh eating lime
that to say the velocity
of ancient stone in permanent song
that to say the body
the blink and the lidless lid
and me the lid closed
to dance the dance
within on the side
without need the lid
to dance the laic's dance
in a circle [' Cocteau try it! '] on
each step a mystery
that to say each an undone stitch
soaked in essential that to say descending
spirals in ascending fluid helix healed
into helicoid that to say opened
into a third minimal superficy

heaved as by rotation
out of lumbar infraficies
outdone by each other done in
precise successions such as you
wouldn't take unnoticed
notice of of being
of a matter that to say
manner of all matters being
in medias res
that to say that maybe that
prius in sensu
that read from a book
that fell open to a page
from another book
torn out folded over
tucked in first that
to say former so double
the weight and cause:
pause : : that's to say
cause which page
to out the all that to say fall
if not so much as open
onto as folded into coincidence
as such such as
you mutatis mutandis
to go ahead and name a few
wouldn't dream of of
being an absolutely frictionless

and featureless force
of association that binds like mad
wind in flames of faux flame
of : pause : : call it : recollection
posing as irreducible irreduct-
ion in unindictable interdict-
ion that to say fact as fate that
to say pure chance that
to say the sanguine
dance without matched exact
to the texture of
the lid on what's within
that to say no matter the matter
of discrepant luster that to say
of isolate sheen on adjectival skin
to say in the mirror of the mirror
of the into in the into
that to say when as in when
in the dream you wouldn't dream
a young man sidles up
sidles back sidles forth again
and back again and to the wings
at right past you and to wings
left and back and he:
pointing over your head he : :
those hands you made
when you did guns
as a boy remember those hands

you did when you made
guns as a boy? And me : _____ :
And in the dream I mean me : _____ :
I mean but sure I did :
and he: pointing both hands
he made to imitate
guns I did near to his
visibly throbbing ventriculars
he : : and letting guns
I made fall invisible into
air he did and making both
guns like I did into
hands like he made into
harp strokes
down like hungry ribs
with his fingers : : : and left
with a two-beat sift
in the sound the vascular
math of this : :
[silence : pause : : which
isn't quote enough for a recess
so don't be quote cute
with yourself and foolish
with your life]
: : : and he : apart from all
collision of incisions
that to say apart from all
collusions of allusion

that to say apart from all
what iridescent froth and avalanche
of detail as
from Ireneo Funes el Memorioso
and in what chronic spasm of risorius
so set forth by the human
cinema of
suave mari mango
considered apart from all
that that that that
to say *exactly that* that to be
apart from all that
is exactly that to be
a part of all this and all that to say it :
that it : and he : my brand new
red Japanned leather
jacket has pockets
pockets in the satin
satin stitched in the inside
inside unstitched in the outside
: and : he
pointing back over
your head : he : : in precise size
and shaped just like those
you did as a boy
in the mirror of the mirror
doing that thing you made
as a boy into the into of the into

with your hands
but still even in the prefect pocket
perfect red of this dream
you wouldn't watch it it being
a fact of that it that
without model without
one one is forced to work
from memory within which one
one is maybe near two
but without still and within which
one one forced to hold back
that it to say freefall
forward it that to say fall out
of the all without
and into the all within all that it but you
most likely wouldn't
imagine that it it that being a matter of time
which from time blessed
to fortune failed that it being a matter
of an instant of insistent instants
and without a watch to watch
within without which one must be to be
within it that that it to say the correct
and convex complex of insistent
instants and yet it that that it goes without
saying it that that it that it to say
all that it that and this shit being itself
of minute and granular

aspect blown into the mute
collapse and vast vastness of chance
that's so
so smooth smooth as dance
dance as to bristle-border on
on border-bristle on all this it that fall within and without
the all but you you wouldn't even think it it being a matter so small

NOOK AND BOON (OF ROCK & HARD PLACES): "CONTEMPLATION"

In scoped and torn cartilage
of key joints, of bent presence, I wonder.

Is this house emptied by the music
of McCoy Tyner playing the keys
like, one by one,
they fell off on the floor, I wonder.

Or did it always sound, I mean beneath
the sound, this way?

The frozen
torrent of your fallen voice,
what I hear when I can't hear it,
slipstream in your fingers
and I'm already beyond
the reach of what ruptured gauze
lovers become when they let the world stand in
for what's between them.

That
private prayer to the public.

Vacuum
sucked into a solitary hand,
at work like a spider over prey,
at a brass buckle.

Secrets.

Puncture wounds
in the private.

Light speed slowed
to a year's length of seven tones
of gold ringed on a slender,
slippery, sex finger.

Let the moon index
the carnivorous applause of children
stomping their endless feet on our limits.

Okay.

They win.

So, I push play
on purpose and Joe Henderson's
sound—but if I didn't say it you'd say it was Trane
so I'm not sure whose sound it is—
fills the house and it's all blown
empty as anything again.

So empty
it could be anybody—which is to say
I could be nobody—living here.

Empty as what follows a physical presence
that moves slower than how, slow-er
than how the bloom
of frontal lobe pushed a thick toe
down past the arch past the heel
that became palm slow as that toe,
pushed by protein blackened
over found-flame, swiveled
its 30 degrees, and curved its back into thumb.

The way our fall thru epics
resembles flight, like parachuters
filmed by parachuters filming other parachuters;
but it's not flight.

A way of mass falling.

Score and chart of how everything leans thru
itself into Higgs boson & how momentum
sprung the trapped math of velocity
into real world collisions.

Life.

I wonder about how
the origin of all how,
for instance, of how the how we hold
tools & exactly what tools became, and how,

of what became human
hands.

    I wonder rooms we built, dim-bruised
on a pre-ancestral shadow down
on an as-yet-unwounded knee.

    What became first cup for water from a pool
clear as stone-showered, lightning lit
mind of song.

    Rooms sharp & slashed
by thrust-pulse, laid waste to
before spheres of starlight ceased to fall
in metallic sheets like high plains hail.

    Damp as a baby's tousled head
& unclaimed as his one hollowed-out eye
open in sleep.

    Forever-blown
dust from a stolen mummy's manicure
holding a space bleached open
in a cat's skull.

    Maybe first cup had to be
broken skull?

The story of origins written
in cursive over blown-out candles.

Don't move when I float
over you unhinged with the motive,
the weapon, the occasion,
and the deliberate weight of a lazy left eye.

And I wonder where you are
and I wonder why, why
you and I wonder why won't why you refuse
to come with me thru twenty hard-spun
door frames of now.

Yes
the terror tastes like the only fact,
the fact of endlessness, and yes, yes, yes
damn the self-fucked infinity
of dream-never.

I told him I'd dreamt
of watching loons javelin
their routes beneath my nude reflection
on the surface of Paradox Lake.

It's in New York, just off I-87 North.

He said he doubted prosaic dream reports
& I pocketed the co-pay and snuck
out the side door with pills prescribed for someone
named Geoffrey McBride.

The strangler on the loose
leaves his blue wind-breaker,
signed "Security" across the back,
at the scene.

I read it on the crawl along the bottom
of the screen in the waiting room.

Say it.

Let's let it all let's let
never never happen again & again to us,
to us which is to say to anyone
who'll come within an echo of themselves
in the dark nickel mirror of a storm cloud
where a lover's face slipped from our hands
& fell from the sky into someone
else's life.

You say "which sky?" & point
at random with murderous arms
of a clocktower reigning on a mute village.

You can say sky, any sky, is only sky
if you want to.

Say it, sky, day &
night, say it, sky, sky, if you must.

Blow a hole thru them all
with your pistol and hang them
from a key ring.

I say it's time to will past the mark,
red-slashed X on the rotten door
and admit ourselves into what secrets
we built.

Admit
the orchestra of spiders who spin
live nerves across the numb streak in our paths.

Ever wonder where now lives
saber tooth, or mammoth tusk?

Look closer.

The evolution of scale.

Now.

Walk thru the unseen morning
web and they ride your shoulder
to work.

They spend the day
in your hair and take up wherever
you left off.

Experts in the invisible sutures
practitioners of the intricate
structure of necessity, what everyone needs:

to be anyone—which is to say what's us
can have nothing to do with us—
needs to live:

to harvest what's lost,

to catch what was invisible til yesterday,
til just now, til slower than how,

to
claim what's dead, blown from our skin
by this mad wind and held before our eye in new light.

CROSSCURRENTS ACROSS

—for A.C.R.

I.

Crouched at a thread-thin stream cross this high-granite dome
above the burnt forest   day fallen gray   a murmur below
a noose of moss-steam   or blue smoke   encircles
snakes my left ankle   high above   a hawk glows red

as illumined   as ensnares

beyond that   a jet leaves its silence
in a white twirl   cirrus scar of vapor

II.

Let's listen to the pilot from the near future:

when we arrive at the gate   please remain
seated   we'll applaud and allow
the citizens to exit the aircraft first
citizens : we at Inter-Personal Air thank you for your service

III.

thanks for risking   by this we mean for saving
your   and by this we mean our   children's lives
by showing them life's living tendons   for enrolling them in the public
schools   in the permeable truth
of the private   truths   for transfusions
incalculable   we thank you

for preoccupations postponed   obsessions   in order   enough
to act in roles   fibrous   in the social fabric   torn and tattered burlap
veterans of real excitement   perennial losers
of potato sack races   survivors
of life and death decisions: sun or shade
for any and all what you refused
to withhold   refuse to refuse   for what must be altered
harp-fused at the Furies' altar   Crane the operator
with the scale on the scale

Evans echoes Evans
"Peace Piece" played over "Flamenco Sketches"

call it : flamenco echoes   [now playing: Channel M on the headset]

for calling a dead cat on the line a dead cat on the line
rare amateurs all   for daring the passion
& maturity of teachers cir-
cumferencing   trial-by-firing the professional

traveling salesman
in us all   foundational anti-elixirists

staring down the mayor and his boss the president and his boss
who won't step from the shadows

for engineers of instigations who lead with their chins
for best friends capable of what's necessary
of feeling out just
beyond the fingertips of what's possible
of walking each other away from the mercenary
the recruiter parked under a tree
in her uniform of national
indelibility in her noondayblue Shelby Mustang
outside the weekday matinee

the handshake that hides a snake

for all partisans in the war on best friends
on what infects connection
for making comb-time
for taking pains   checking the neighbor's daughter's scalp
for the blight beetle's bite

for doing what felt needed when the world of flame screamed:
your name your name your name your name / whispered [in your
      voice] :
'you're wasting your [meaning their] time'

on the off chance we've a poet on board one whom
hasn't fingered prayer beads and chanted
to the gods of nine-times-out-of-ten   we thank you for alternatives
to the faux-spark of short-circuited neuroses

voiceless verb-jolts of suburban exiles   for tonal alternatives
to the haunted and empty lust
for *privilege*   yes.   for marrow alternatives

to all click-in-box clones of :
neda ulaby   fred jones   zöe chase   daphne blake
[and brother beige we've not forgotten you] for serum to verbal death
by cocktail : zip / bracket / income /
code : sat / gre : Guantanamo: Scooby Doo we mean no offense
we've all had colleagues

[voice-over] : *r-run r-raken*

Whoever you are wherever you are from
un-stupified not unhappy   Citizens who stood up blind dates
with priceless Wi-Fi and found themselves
together in a red velvet corner of the hotel bar
reading the same paragraph of Victor Serge   over and over
to each other

"I can think about nothing now but power. Truth stripped of
its metaphysical poetry, exists only in the brain. Destroy a few
brains, quickly done! Then, goodbye truth."

a falling together of accomplices
& over we thank you for your problematic verve-ness   energy
to face consequences
of bone-faith heresy and worm-toothed truths necessary
for thefts
of time—the *kind* of time—it took to walk her kids to bus stop
turnstile school gate

For nine-year-old Matthew's AIDS-wracked fallen bird of a mama
out there upstate   racket wrist taped   spindle ankle   afterschool at the park
along the river   living and   failing living trying
to play tennis with the boy

for Matthew   age 11   at the park by himself staring at the Amtrak bridge :
"that one the Empire Express…" : "that one the Ethan Allen…"

those who steer   have learned to   steer by elbow-nudge   quick jog
and riff-glance without the selfless
fundamentalisms of Clarity & Obliquity   for: soulflesh   nervedash
[   ]
take eleven syllables : we trust you with the open line above

who have learned not to know but   follow a lead in the precision
of loose measures   the scales of lunar notes   overhead
facts underfoot   in attention to the wane-blur
of what wax'd in the pull on clear fluid in the spine

IV.

the cool mountain heat   thirsty air takes sweat from the ribbon-slice
of sun on my throat   thread of mirror cuts the stone
reflected   the tendril's path across
& off   skybath   a million diagonals
tangent my denim shoulder

salt   impossible jet overhead   war down below   all around
people crazed
in midnight theaters   unsure of why they are there
Premiere of *Batman* in Colorado

    [text into chaos: where r u ? : blood on my coat & don't know whose]

unsure who   unsure if   unsure what   unsure   finally   because they were told
were assured   it would hurt   if it really happened   to them

    [text from chaos : behind fire trucks : not sure I can feel my legs]

V.

[verbatim itineraries in globalized segregation   ]

The nuclear aircraft carrier, U.S.S. John C. Stennis, patrols the Persian Gulf. I saw a report of this with news of Syria's intensifying civil war. The carrier was being repositioned to exert an American presence in the Syrian conflict. The name Stennis caught my eye. I remembered it from history and from Baldwin's *No Name in the Street* so I looked up the reference:

> Let us tell it like it is: the rhetoric of a Stennis, a Maddox, a Wallace, historically and actually, has brought death to untold numbers of black people and it was meant to bring death to them.

The commercial on TV ends with an aerial photograph of a carrier passing through the screen. The image fades into the message printed where the ship had been a moment ago:
The U.S. Navy: A Global Force For Good
in some the note   100% On Watch   boils up out of the ship's turbulent wake in the water

In the fall of 2012 I moved with my son, Milan, to Cambridge, MA for a fellowship. The day before we left Athens, GA, during the first week of class at the university, I found myself a block from campus, in the middle of the downtown, staring at the Georgia Heritage Flag which features the Confederate insignia. I photographed the scene in the street to take it with me to Massachusetts. As I stood beneath the flag flying outside a bar, two young black men walked past. I gestured to them and they paused. I waved up at the flag and said, "Can you believe this shit?" They smiled, waved me off, "Man, that's just noise."

VI.

Noise. Or is that noize? Like Stennis's rhetoric. Like "A Global Force For Good." Like 1960: Mingus and Dolphy in "The Original Fables of Faubus," a surreal skit of twelve toned harmonics and loaded up with an energy linked to those who haven't tuned out the noise. In 2014, OG Maco leers into the camera in his video for "U Guessed It," warning: "I'm still in that *place*." That place made of noise and its endless echoes. That flesh and blood place verges on another place where the body is the verge of the bars on the windows where its temperature verges to the cold steel drawer and its rollers.

Garion Morgan is also called No Noize, an Oakland dancer in a blaze orange windbreaker. Hood up. Bandana across the bridge of his nose. *Turf Feinz*.

And when Mssr Maco says "still" it sounds like "steel" to me, I'm steel in that place, call it a Fanon-ian slip, and I think I first learned the name Richard Russell because it appears in the roll call of "Nazi Fascist Supremes" run down by drummer Dannie Richmond as cued by Mingus, on bass, in their mock-live recording of "The Original Fables of Faubus." They recorded it on Candid Records because Columbia wouldn't record the lyrics. It might be true that, later in his 40-year career in the U.S. Senate representing Georgia, Richard B. Russell wasn't quite the vicious radical racist that Stennis was. Or possibly, it's the reverse. Steel in *his* place, Mingus didn't care... His chest tattooed with flowers, OG Maco licks his lips with the tip of his tongue and chimes in my ear: "You'se mother-fucking right."

VII.

When I returned to Athens from Cambridge in late 2012 I found
that the university's new, Parthenon-style Special Collections Library
had been completed and named after Richard B. Russell. This made
me curious. Visiting a historian friend in Durham, we checked his
collection for notes about Russell's role in the Southern bloc and as co-
author of the "Southern Manifesto" from 1956.

During his first term in office, Russell is quoted to have said the
following:

> Any Southern white man worth a pinch of salt would give his all
> to maintain white supremacy, and it is a disgrace that some would
> constantly seek to drag the negro issue into our primaries where as a
> matter of fact they do not participate and can not . . . As one who was
> born and reared in the atmosphere of the Old South, I am willing to
> go as far and make as great a sacrifice to preserve and insure white
> supremacy in the social, economic, and political life of our state as any
> man who lives within her borders . . . Should some real menace from
> the negro present itself, I still believe that the white manhood of not
> only Georgia, but the entire South, would rise en masse immediately
> and assert itself again.

As OG Maco's "U Guessed It" verges on 9 million YouTube views,
in October 2014, Erykah Means writes in "he scare the hell outta me
when he do that 'HUWAH' thing." I looked back in December and
he had passed 14 million views. I think how much in our bodies, our

action, our syntax is somewhere, simulated-somehow somewhere
gunfire. You blinked. The page goes black and another somewhere
simulated somewhere shot goes off.

VIII.

One day a while ago I dropped Stacey at work so I could take her Honda to the dealer for service. Phil Hughes Honda. Unaccustomed to that route, I asked my phone for directions. Siri answered that she had no listing for "Feel Hughes Honda."

In December 2014, in the wake of the Michael Brown and Eric Garner grand jury decisions, protests flare in Berkeley, students block the Amtrak route, crowds in Missouri and New York City and Chicago block traffic and my friend from Oakland texts to say that his aunts worry protests will raise the price of groceries for them. Meanwhile, officials in Ramallah disagree over the cause in the death of a Palestinian Minister Zaid Abu Ein. Not yet awake, 6:15 AM on the eleventh, I hear, as if underwater, the radio news note that one autopsy listed signs of hemorrhaging due to throat compression. Sound moves faster underwater than in the air, I know that. And, I know, at that velocity, the ears tell the human brain that sound reaches them both at once and so the brain tells us we're surrounded.

IX.

And, I remember Bellow's Herzog wondering if he really has to think about killing people in order to remain sane.

Mingus chants, "Why's he so sick and ridiculous?" OG Maco points his invisible weapon, "HUWAH." Erica Means, wherever she is, ducks for cover as his figure explodes in static, his shape filled with electric, cartoon colors.

And I know it's good sense to go with no noize. Otherwise, we give our lives to these people who don't even want to be people. But, I look around me at the people and their postures. Their figures. On the bus, when they walk, when they drive. I wonder the costs of the energy it takes not to notice. And, how, if one—and everyone—determines not to notice the noize, I wonder what else falls into that numbness and the scent I wonder of sweat, or of I wonder blood, when it comes back out of the pores. Pain measured in blood pressure; fear and rage (and grief) in glycemic index. And here you might think I'm talking about a tradition (which is not your fault) when, really, I've been driving my life up against the white wall of the wherewithall.

Let us tell it like it is: the rhetoric of a . . . was meant to bring death to them.

X.

United Nations stammers along   a confused hierarchy
of Arsenals   shaken   at best an unstable solution   last night

the stammer of midterm elections drones   overhead

dream-dust on the olive   rumor of vermouth & raised up
over the clean swipe

of the barwoman's cloth : another man sits down   he's a white man
he wants to talk
to talk to me without
talking   too much you haven't said   partner
finished saying will ever say   begun now
if I get your gesture right
and now here you are   somewhere
and you talk to me   your eyes full of it

talking to me and you say you want to talk to me   about silence

XI.

I could feel her letting go   packing up details   uncharacteristic endings
a line left off   frayed   (and now if I spoke to her)
could feel you
staring over the edge   down   and I didn't know what to do

knew there was something always
lost in nothing to do   always something done

could sense an updraft moving a near-visible web
in the space ajar   the un-inhaled word   hospice
and qualifiers (temporal) twisting in the breath (yours) :
in the doorway to what [was soon to be] was (ours)

we'd agreed without agreeing long long ago   cooperations made
explicit in acts   hand in hand   in heads leaned against
the brick wall beside us   sun on
the table top strewn with banal questions   answers upturned
in eyes focused on what appears
after vanishing and bright as two glasses
of noonday'd and sunray'd chardonnay

agreed to converse along any living vein   even thinned to infinite
thinned thin as this
mirror-ribbon across the stone dome
even if blank at the center agreed

to train focus in peripheries of living time   possible visions   determined
(your) : "enlarge the font and re-send   please   I'll use my eyes for what matters"
agreed to locate possible centers
shared between us made of frayed edges within us

within us between us / us between us within   [/ = mirror]

that yet-to-be word for bulletproof   refraction
that articulation in arms
around each other   power in reflection

and arms around means torn away   we knew that we knew that
had long agreed with Miles
so what   avoided that dependence
on Rilke   intolerance
of the particular   these aren't angels   friend

if there's spiced calf kidney and Spanish onion
on the breath   a speck of midtown
basil over your tooth   cabernet along the gum-line in full laughter
and love's human pull
against the clock reigning above the bright night
sky of the city :
(my) last dash from the lobby four minutes
ahead of the last train north : (your) bottom lip poked out
(your) "be good   friend   but not too good"
and exhorting the cab driver   now (your) other to (my) some

where   now   soon   love   more
(yours) Outward   militant : "enough   I've taken Antonio as far as he can go"
And these two

of us one last : always a more : always a soon

XII.

and the thread-mirror drops off the granite and evaporates long
before it joins   ijaz   immutable
the topaz lens   convex of crystal cornea
in the rust-bottomed lake   the warmth of the stone goes fibrous goes
shirt goes into my faded-blue back   breeze in the arch
music is the two-beat rhythm
of my friend's book on my belly   pulse on the page between
chapters   the silent sheet of sound
a swollen knuckle of love   that's no failure
fits behind my ear
echoes in the bald-pulse
of my head against my pack   and poems go
the way light goes down arrayed by the silicic structure
of the lake   visible as to what goes on

in the space above   and what lives beneath the skin
skein of last year's needles
of pine   amid itself attuned   in unprecedented concert
in taste   in the way that taste sounds   volume : the only precision :
the first the knife-slice   upward
of apple against a thumb : in the way one says what one

says   says : well   we'll play it by ear

& learning always listens somehow &
hears someone somehow
else in its listening somehow   else in its listening learns nothing

in my mouth in saline liquid in salt on the slice   near-in the sensual
texture of an insensate border   in-near the mirror in-given play of
light in newborn in silt

PHONEME DEATH

New science says we humans are unable, ever, to really see anyone whose face differs beyond a certain limit from the original visual ingredients— templates that take shape in relation to faces that come close to us in the first weeks of life—of our perceptions. Same applies to phoneme death. Our ability to hear and distinguish upwards of 840 sounds at birth drops down to between 20 and 40 distinct sounds by six months of age. The voices and faces that come near us in early life reinforce patterns, destroy others, and author the basic premises of sight and sound into our lives. Apparently, the Japanese and Xhosa languages lead the world with an average of around 43 durable phonemes. No matter how many languages we learn, before we know a word in any of them, we undergo untold hemorrhages in our auditory capacity. These losses translate themselves into the muscles of our mouths. These losses behind our eyes encode themselves in everything we see. Studies show the brain doesn't trust this blindness. It writes suspicion into the way the tone of someone's voice plays silence in our ears. Yet, the mysteries have an allure. Somewhere our psyche knows it has been islanded off, at some level, beyond the reach in sight or sound of any visitor who comes down the road. Maybe this is where poems come from? From the urge to enter a pre-hemorrhage zone where, we must sense from somewhere, our human, pre-individual capacity to see, to hear, to trust, remains wider than this narrow thing we've become. In a poem, a kind of music happens and we see ourselves, somehow, through the blindness of others.

VERBATIM ROUTES: JANUARY 3, 2004

Croatia. I'm a few days past 37 years old. Surely this place knows me better than I know it. I've been here twenty-five years ago but it'd be hard to call that me. My grandmother, my father's mother (b. Maria Starchović by then married to Ivan Pavlić), left here in the late '20s to meet her seldom-seen husband in Québec. Two kids in tow: my Aunt Mary, now 90, living in Vancover, B.C.; and my Uncle John who lived his life in Trail, B.C. where they all grew up, and where he stayed until he shot himself in 1986. I don't know by what route my grandmother left here but it must have been something like the reverse of how I arrived. Over the mountain from the coast, into the snow. Thru Hrelijin, thru Fujina. My father and I are on our way to the village his parents grew up in. I turn the Fiat off the highway across the surf of drifts arranged by the wind. Wind. Chicago was supposed to be windy. The Bura of northern Croatia turn over cars, close bridges, blow families of Adriatic bear across the bay to Krk ("keerk"), Cres (closer to "thresse" than "Kress" but, to say the word, you have to place an "l" tongue flutter between the t and h to make the "r" do what it's supposed to do). This region is called Gorsky Kotar. This is where I come from. So I'm told.

Last night my father took me to a diner, Bujan's ("Boo-yan's"),
pitched on a cliff outside Hrelijin, ten miles of switchbacks from and
a thousand meters above the Kvarner Bay in the Adriatic. I'd guess
someone had chiseled it into that particular nook of rock because some
concave-convexity in the shape of the cliff created a chance downdraft
that held the building to Earth. Apart from inscrutable geophysics, it
seemed like an unlikely outpost upon which to put a diner. The wind
strafes us both between the car and the front door. I hold on to the old
man, all five-foot six of him, who leads the way.

The place is packed. Groups of loud-talking people, families. Single, silent men at small tables, truckers. Bujan, the owner, greets my father, "Ay-edie, Ay-edie..." grabs his hand and speak-whistles somethingsomethingsomething that means, elaborately, "welcome!" in Croatian. Bujan sits us down at a long table (also packed) outside the dining room and returns with a tray of colored bottles. He solemnly pours into a tiny cup from a green bottle, picks up a red one and fills the other tiny cup, puts his big hand on my shoulder and hands me a shot of homebrewed, flammable syrup. He laughs a helium laugh that sounds like it comes from some huge, angular bird that hunts shallow water for food. My father somethings-something to Bujan, and then, I think repeating himself, he flicks out his hands like he's about to catch a basketball passed from me, and says, "my son." "Son!," Bujan whistle-says to me and half the coast, "You *look* like you're from Gorsky Kotar!" his laugh, "hooaloo, hooaloo, hooaloo!" My father stares at me with a satisfaction that seemed arranged to include both of us. For him, which is to say, for us, this is very unusual. The wind tears at the windows. Still hooalooing, Bujan fills our glasses from another bottle. Bitter-looking truck drivers in stiff black leather jackets turn from leaning over their ashtrays, coffee saucers and drinks poured from still other colored bottles full of berries and herb stalks. Bujan somewhere-elses himself in a flash. My father turns, watching Bujan disappear and then he laughs. My thought: I don't think I've heard that laugh in English. Then he turns and stares at me with a look open enough for me to walk inside it, arrange the furniture, and sit wherever I want. I *know* I've never seen *that* look in English. He doesn't say anything to me just then, this is common enough in English. I speak no Croatian at all.

A voice calls to me from the back of my brain: Summer, 1990. I was 25. I'd been living with my girlfriend and another roommate on Avenue C in Manhattan. In truth, I don't know why I was there. It was the first summer that I hadn't worked with the bricklayers since 1985. Instead of carrying acid-proof mortar around in a steel mill, I spent every other day reading all the books on Yorùbá culture I could request at the Schomberg Center Library in Harlem. The circular reading room. Reading was a new space for me and I was extremely careful— call it paranoid—about what I put in it. Most days there was another man who arrived after me. He wore a full camouflaged uniform with a foot-long bowie knife in a sheath strapped to his leg. One day I met a very nice woman at the library entrance. It turned out she was Paula Giddings. I held the door for her and she thanked me and asked my name. I told her my name and, after she entered, I followed her inside. I liked why-am-I-hereing, broke, in New York City very much. Odd days I stayed downtown, played basketball in Tomkins Square Park before it was occupied by the NYPD, fenced off, and closed down for the rest of the summer.

One day, I was walking in Harlem, toward Lenox Avenue and approaching 116th Street on a bombed-out block within sight of the avenue. Nearing the corner, a bowtie and bean-pie'd Nation of Islam member began attempting to sell me a copy of *The Final Call*. "A dollar, brother, one dollar," he began. He said the price in a falling, mourning tone of voice, as if the price itself was an ironic crime. Sorry, man, don't have a dollar, just this subway token. It was true enough; I didn't have enough money to carry any of it on blocks like that in Harlem in 1990 where here and there you could feel space sizzle and see the air crack. I had some change. He continued, "sev-en-ty five cents!" Like I said . . . By now we're approaching the station steps, he's walking backward facing me. "Fifty cents, for the righteous truth, brotherman, fif-ty cents." His tonal invocation of the price of truth, an ironic crime, had become an objective, historical outrage. His face close to mine, a small delta of red veins flows in one eye, a constellation of freckles across the bridge of his nose. His eyes looked tired. I didn't pause. I turned from him to head downstairs to the train. "25 cents, Blackman, if you just *say* you'll read it . . ." I turn to make sure he's talking to me. We're face to face, again. Okay, I'll read it, sure. I handed the suited man a quarter and took the paper down the steps.

I was flipping thru the ironies and historical outrages of the exchange in my head when I approached the turnstile. Nothing focused. My mind was still aboveground on the street as I attempted to find the slot to put my token in a twisted post of shredded metal. I don't know if I took a step back but the lens of my vision widened. From there I could see that the line of turnstiles had been decimated. I'd jumped turnstiles on a few desperate nights in Brooklyn already that summer. Instinctively, I looked for the token-booth person, the booth was likewise smashed, empty. This widening of vision must have occurred very quickly, because only then did a person walk past me, in rhythm, stepping over the ruined barrier and onto the platform. At that instant, I noticed a little boy with intricate graffiti shaved into his haircut sitting on the bent post to the far right. My "$.25 *Black*man..." copy of *The Final Call* tucked under my arm, my backpack on my back, I smiled at the little boy and motioned, "what happened... ," with my hands. And he, stepping off and turning his back to me: "just walk in what is you stupid?" I did. I wasn't. Or maybe I was?

I look back across Bujan's moonshine-bottle-strewn table doubting there's enough room in my father's newly open stare for even this moment's lightning of association, not in any language. I'm probably wrong. But, I didn't then have the language for such accommodations. My father never went to high school, began work as an apprentice bricklayer at Kiminko Smelter in Trail, British Columbia in 1945. Moved to Chicago in 1955 and worked for the next 35 years for a wage. A good wage. Each minute of his wage-earning time was earned against the physical exertion of his body. According to his fellow workers, men not given to inflated views of one another, he was very skilled, worked with a specialized kind of industrial brick. So, each moment of his earning-time, as it is said, "every penny of it," also came via a high-powered, problem-solving intellect located somewhere between his body and the skill of his craft. Historically speaking, he was well paid. Somewhere around $25/hour in the 1980s when I worked with the same small company he did, National Acid Proofing, located on the South Side of Chicago. Historically speaking, he worked hard. And, historically speaking, in his mind, he was doing so so that his wife and kids could live a life different from his. This gives my father a kind of intensely coherent and deeply limited authority in the world. His world. The man knows where his feet are on the ground. I'm definitely his son. During my life, he was almost never home, two weeks per year, unless he was out of work. Owing to the specialized brick and the constant travel, he was rarely out of work. It was always tense in the house when he was, his minute-by-minute confrontation with history postponed, trapped in the house he was paying for as part of the pitched battle. By 2003, my father was done with the United

States, which is exactly to say, he was done working. My parents moved, for him almost "back," to Croatia. A country, he calls it "the old country," that was, at that time, approaching ten years old.

When my father was little, they lived in a mining town, Rossland, British Columbia, about five miles up a mountain from the Columbia River. He remembers his father was working in the smelter on the river and his mother was putting something, biscuits, in the oven. And, he asked, "Was it like this in the old country," though he wouldn't have said that in English. And she : his translation : "if it was like this in the old country, we'd never have left." His mother spoke halting English, at best. Maybe I saw her four times. When I asked her something it was never clear to me if she didn't know the answer or didn't understand the question. She had no teeth, and no false teeth, her face would curl into a closed fist. She'd shake her head in a way lost between frustration at her English and pity at my dependence upon it, and reply, "no, me no fine it." She had three daughters, two died. One, Irene, died of fever from a wood tick when she was two. The other, Helen, died of an appendicitis when she was 18. I'd never known the names of my father's dead sisters. Recently, his brother, Willie, a retired bricklayer who lives in Seattle, showed me a rare photo with everyone in it and pointed everyone out. When he said the names of the sisters who died, I felt something strange pass through me. I looked up at Willie's wife, Helen. And, then my mind followed the thing passing through and I thought of my suicided uncle John's wife, Irene. It's strange enough, to me, that two brothers would find wives with the names of their dead sisters. It's even stranger that no one had ever talked about it. This second strangeness, possibly, accounts for the density of the fog, maybe even the velocity of the wind. Later, when I mentioned it, my father told me that John's wife was actually named Eileen. And, he said they really never knew if his little sister's name was Irene or Eileen because his mother named her, in English, and she could neither hear nor pronounce the difference between the two names.

This Bura could blow us from here to there and on to somewhere else. It whistles in the plastic case around the driver's rearview mirror, jerks the car so that, from time to time, I'm afraid it'll turn over. I steer into each diagonal drift that traverses the road. It feels as much like sailing as driving. We thread our way through the valley in January 2004. Past the pulp mill where Veilco and Pavle and Sonja work, so I'm told. Past cars stopped to put on chains. Two men with black coats flapping open like broken wings tie down the hood of their dented blue Opal wagon with yellow rope. We drive under the high rail-bridge that Ruza ("Roojah"), daughter of my great-uncle Paul, helped the Partisans "drop" (so I'm told) in '43 so the Nazis and Ustashe couldn't get trains to Rijeka, the largest city on the northern coast. I learn Rijeka is the Croatian word for river. I learn this because Ruza still calls Rijeka "Fiume." Many of the places in this part of Croatia still bear Italian names (at least in the minds of villagers) from occupations that began with the Venetians. Here's the sign for the village where my grandparents were born: LIĆ. So, there's the name: Pav-Lić. Paul of Lić. At this point, my father is visibly uncomfortable at something, he says it's my driving, which I doubt. He announces: "So, here's where you're from, how does it feel?" I don't know the word, if there is one, so I don't say anything. I drive ahead while the white surf striates the road.

Ruza speaks Italian and Croatian. She speaks no English at all. She's lived in Lić over 80 years. My father says she told him about one winter when she was a girl, before the war. His mother and his sister were still living in the house. His older brother was a baby. The sleet and wind froze the cow solid. Standing up. Alive. Bell and all. Her job was to comb the hill for sticks and brush. They built small fires around the cow and blocked the wind with their bodies. She lived. Hair singed, milk spoiled. They cooked with goat's milk. I imagine Ruza laughing and imitating the cow's voice from inside the ice. At dinner, she and I rarely speak but everyone else does. My father, talks. He laughs. He even sings? The pool of silence around Ruza reminds me of the silence at my grandparents dinner table. No talk. Just toothless slurpings and the two-beat, rasp-rhythm of the pepper mill turning the surface of the barley and bean soup black. I notice Ruza never uses her napkin and it remains folded at the side of her plate. Everyone else's napkins have disappeared beneath the table. Except mine, I'm always nervous at tables like this so I forget the napkin thing and then realize it's making it all worse. My cousins here call her Baca Ruza with a thick, percussive affect I translate as reverence. She's dressed in an elegant sweater and gold locket, she says nothing, smiles, eats for two and wipes the corners of her mouth with each bite of bread.

Down the road from the house, this is the house my grandfather, Ivan, and his brother Paul, were born in, I don't know what's before that. Up the road there's a stone church where the Virgin Mary appeared to the villagers in the snow one Easter morning during the war. My father points to the wall of the church where Nazis and Ustashe executed any Partisans they could find. Up the frozen slope from the church, what's left of 'Gypsy Hill,' a few stone foundations. My father tells me the villagers say they found it burnt down and empty one morning in '44, smoke still coming from the blackened stones of the chimneys. I wonder if that was before or after the Virgin Mary appeared? It's bad either way. "Found it burnt and empty," I think; I've got my doubts. I walk around the corner and whisper it to the wind. The wind bites my face. And, up behind the house, the cave where Ruza hid with her father Paul Pavlić paratrooper, Canadian, radical journalist and unionist. Camp X. Exiled provocateur. My father says he remembers, when he was a kid, the Mounties coming to the house to ask about his uncle and that they were told to say nothing. He says it was easy, because they didn't know anything. By whatever name, it was the first Paul and his daughter had ever seen of each other. She didn't find out who he was until after the war was over. Earlier that day, Pavle, my cousin, hands me a photo of Ruza, in a black skirt, 16 years old. She stands in the snow, smiling, proudly holding her machine gun. This is the silent woman dabbing her mouth with bread across the table from me.

A few years later, of course, tables turned. Partisans lined up any
retreating Nazis they could catch along the same wall at the church.
Ruza bound their wrists, you're told. And led them before the stones.
The men did all the shooting at executions.

At the church, I stand at the wall, inches around the corner from the sheer blade of wind. The Bura whistles past the huge faces in the corner stones of the church. My fingers fit perfectly in the pockmarks left by the bullets. Fossil glove or empty grey eyes. For a second, I wonder which holes are which, which stones bear which names. I wonder if it matters? Wars. I remember the first time I was here. "Yugoslavia." I was 11. About the same age "Croatia" is now. My favorite part of the trip: tidal pools of the Adriatic, and games of "Pong" for six Dinar a piece. *Roots* was on the tiny screen in the stove-heated kitchen. *Roots* in Lić. Pavle was maybe six? Each time he saw me, he pointed and called, "Amey-dikan, Amey-dikan." I remember he and his brother Goran watching the TV laughing and repeating "Kunta-Kenta." In his room, upstairs, now, his army boots still have mud on the heels. He said there are villages up-country, in Lika, in Jezera, still populated only by sheep. So, I gather the question of "which stone is which" still matters to someone. "They're still there," he says, "at least the ones we didn't eat while we guarded their empty villages."

It's a country of stones. That much is clear. Of walls and smoke. Even the wind is a wall. Even the walls made of smoke. And, every stone has its own face. I've seen the name, Pavlić, on the gravestones behind the church. And, I think, it can't matter to them which ones are which. Can it? I don't think it matters to me. Though at home, in the U.S. it still feels like life and death as to who is whom, "twenty-five cents, *Black*man..." I hear... And, variations of that echo follow me everywhere I go. They meet me coming up the streets of Athens, GA, a so-called liberal town where, on most streets, in most stores, and most certainly in most churches and homes, Apartheid still patterns life from the surface of the skin downward. This is where I live now. I know most of these walls in Gorsky Kotar were built to clear the ground for crops, or, possibly, to keep the olive trees from making their escape. Fugitives. An upstart olive tree and her saplings, riding the back of a bear across the bay, stowing away on a ferry to Venice. And, I see faces. I turn the corner toward the front of the church, my father's telling me which wall was blown up when and by whom in what war. He might have said why but I lost his voice to the wind when I turned the corner. Faces. I know this one's mine because it burns in the blind wind. "This does burn," I say to myself, though I can't feel my fingers when I touch my cheek. And, I think, maybe that might matter, to someone.

CORRECTION: WESTERN METAPHYSICS (PLATO'S CAVE) REVISED IN INCOGNITO'S "BABY IT'S ALRIGHT"

When I'm reaching for the shadows
With my back against the wall
I can hear your voice in the darkness say . . .

NOTES TO THE TEXT

EPIGRAPHS

Susan Sontag: "Marat/Sade/Artaud" in *Against Interpretation*, p. 169; Adrienne Rich's trans., "XV," *Ghazals of Ghalib*, Ed. Aijaz Ahmad, p. 78; Irma Thomas, "I Need Your Love So Bad," *Sweet Soul Queen of New Orleans: The Irma Thomas Collection*.

DIALECTICS OF LIBERATION ACCORDING TO CARLEEN ANDERSON

p. 1 quotes the song "You Are" from the album *Easy Sunday Soul: Us Edition*.

VERBATIM BREAKING NEWS: MARCH 25, 2011.

p. 9: In an unexpected (by me) and very welcome (certainly to opponents of the death penalty) turn of events, on Friday, July 21, 2015, in Athens, GA, a jury sentenced Jamie Hood to life without the possibility of parole. In my mind, the Black Lives Matter movement and the citizens' footage of and national publicity surrounding the terrifying series of police killings across the nation in 2014 and 2015 certainly had something to do with the jury's decision not to sentence Jamie Hood to death. Even in relation to very recent history, this decision represents a very welcome event in a state which, while Hood awaited trial, executed Troy Davis on September 21, 2011 amid widespread reasonable doubt about the evidence that led to his conviction in 1991. See *I Am Troy Davis*, Jen Marlowe and Martina Davis-Correia, Haymarket Books, Chicago, 2013.

p. 21: Beckett quote from *Watt. Selected Works of Samuel Beckett: Volume 1*. Ed. Paul Auster, p. 375.

p. 26: Jenny Hendrix. "This One is the Whole: Italo Calvino's Letters." *Los Angeles Review of Books*, June 30, 2013. Italo Calvino, *Invisible Cities*, Harcourt, 1973, p. 165.

BECAUSE TRANE WOULD HAVE BEEN 87 TODAY: SEPTEMBER 23, 2013

p. 43: This poem contains echoes within a constellation of information including: epigraph from Jesmyn Ward's *Men We Reap*; Calyx, an archaic term for synapse;

synapse, a gap over which neurons communicate via electricity or chemicals; Hans Held, German physiologist, discovered one of the largest synapses, "the Calyx of Held"; Santiago Ramón y Cajal, Spanish physiologist and painter who proved that the nervous system is not a continuous system and won the 1906 Nobel Prize for Medicine for his "Neuron Doctrine"; Bésos, a river in Barcelona; Coltrane quote at the bottom of pages from Jean Clouzet and Michel Delorme, "Entretien avec John Coltrane," *Les Cahiers du Jazz* 8 (1963), p. 1-14; Juanita Naima was John Coltrane's first wife; Nica is Baroness Pannonica de Koenigswarter; Orrin Keepnews, founder of Riverside Records; Monk, Thelonious Monk; Nellie, Nellie Monk, Thelonious Monk's wife; Termination Shock, point at which the solar wind's velocity falls below the speed of sound; Heliopause, border between the solar system, an envelope of plasma provided by solar wind, and interstellar space; Troy Davis, black man executed in Georgia, despite serious questions as to his guilt, on Sept 21, 2011; *Interstellar Space*, Coltrane's last studio album recorded February 22, 1967; Risë Stevens, lead woman in *The Chocolate Soldier* ca. 1941; Branislaw Kaper (aka Edward Kane) wrote "While My Lady Sleeps" for the movie, *The Chocolate Soldier*; May 31, 1957, while playing with Monk at The Five Spot Café at Cooper Square in Manhattan, Coltrane recorded "While My Lady Sleeps," concluding the song with his first studio-recorded polyphonic note, on *John Coltrane*, his first album as leader, Prestige 7105; band on Prestige 7105: Coltrane (ts), Paul Chambers (b), Albert Heath (d), Johnny Splawn (t), Mal Waldron (p); Bob Weinstock, founder of Prestige Records; "Weinstock method" was to approximate the energy of live performance, foreswear rehearsals, record one full take of a song and move on; Rudy Van Gelder, New Jersey Optometrist and recording engineer for Prestige; Gus Khan, wrote lyrics to "While My Lady Sleeps"; Artie Shapiro, Los Angeles-based bass player, recorded Billie Holiday in rehearsal in his living room August 22, 1955; "5:30 A.M." Adrienne Rich, *Collected Early Poems*, p. 304.

RENDITION OF A PYRRHONIST

p. 55: Eric Holder, 82ND Attorney General of the United States (2009–2014);

[Alberto] Gonzales, 80TH Attorney General of the United States (2005–2007); John Yoo, Deputy Assistant Attorney General under U.S. Attorney General John Ashcroft (2001–2005) during first term of President George W. Bush; Johann Heinrish Ferdinand von Autenrieth founded psychiatric clinic at Tübingen pioneering aggressive restraints and treatments for mental disorders including "Autenrieth's mask"; Friedrich Hölderlin, German romantic poet, at one point was a patient at Tübingen; In *Coercion as Cure: A Critical History of Psychiatry*, Thomas Szasz writes: "The purpose of the Autenrieth mask is emblematic of the aim of all involuntary psychiatric interventions: the silencing of the patient" (77). "But not is it though, time," translation of Hölerlin quoted in Anne Atik's *How It Was: A Memoir of Samuel Beckett*. Atik writes that her husband, the painter Avigdor Arikha, and Beckett quoted this line to each other as a greeting.

p. 56: Samir Khan, American born editor of *Inspire* magazine. Killed on September 30, 2011 in a drone strike while with radical Imam and leader Anwar al-Awlaki in Yemen; The Blue Room is a diner in Mombasa, Kenya; Natalie Webb, alias of Samantha Louise Lewthwaite, aka the White Widow, widow of (7/7) London bomber, Germaine Lindsay.

p. 57: Aafia Siddiqui, Pakastani-born, American educated (M.I.T., PhD Brandeis University) woman now serving 86 years for incident during interrogation while being detained for questioning about her affiliation to (her second husband's uncle) al-Quaeda leader, Khalid Sheikh Mohammed; Salt Pit, a brick factory outside Kabul, Afghanistan, reputed location of a U.S.-run secret prison or "black site" used to detain and question terror suspects without bringing them to U.S. controlled territory; Szmany, Poland, location of one black site.

p. 62: K.C. is short for Kenyan Cowboy, a local term for British ex-pat residents of Kenya.

p. 63: Dana Priest, national security beat reporter for *The Washington Post*. Priest won the 2006 Pulitzer Prize for reporting on black site prisons and other aspects of the U.S. counterterrorism campaign.

VERBATIM PALESTINE: JUNE 3, 2014

p. 65: Epigraph from Etel Adnan's *To Look at the Sea is to Become What One Is: An Etel Adnan Reader*. Eds Thom Donovan and Brandon Shimoda, Nightboat, 2014.

p. 70: Giva't Kharseena, settlement on the outskirts of Hebron / Al-Khalil, in the West Bank.

p. 71: James Baldwin, "Letters from a Journey." *Harper's* (May 1963), p. 48-52.

p. 75: BMF: Black Mafia Family. "Shuttles in the rocking loom of history" is a quote from Robert Hayden's poem "Middle Passage," *Collected Poems*, Liveright, p. 51

p. 76: Etel Adnan, *Of Citites and Women: Letters to Fazzaz*, The Post-Apollo Press, 1993.

p. 79: Roland Barthes's essay, "The Light of the South West," is available in *Incidents*, Seagull Books, 2012, p. 1-16.

p. 82: Yusef Komunyakaa, "Untitled Blues," *Copacetic*. Wesleyan University Press, p. 14.

p. 83: "Ghazal from 7/14/1968" appears in Adrienne Rich, *Collected Early Poems*, p. 342.

WITH WORM FOR WORM THE BIRD: A COSMOLOGICAL FILIBUSTER

p. 88: References to: Jean Cocteau's essay "The Laic Mystery: An Essay in Indirect Criticism, *Pagany* (December 1932); "prius in sensu" comes from The Peripatetic Axiom of Aquinas by way of Aristotle: "Nihil est in intellectu quod non prius in sensu" or "Nothing in the intellect if not first in the senses."; "mutatis mutandis," Latin for "only necessary changes having been made."

p. 92: References to Ireneo in "Funes el Memorioso" a 1942 short story by Jorge Luis

Borges in which the character possesses a perfect photographic memory and is thereby rendered effectively incapable of thinking; "Suave, mari magno" comes from Lucretius De Rerum Natura 2, the lines "Suave, mari magno turbantibus aequora ventis / E terra magnum alterius spectare laborem" or "It is pleasant, when the winds are buffeting the waves on the great sea / to watch from the land the great toil of someone else." The lines wonder about the role of security in the formulation of truth or pleasure.

CROSSCURRENTS ACROSS

p. 107: "Peace Piece," *Everybody Digs Bill Evans* (1958). Bill Evans employs the same chords as those later used in Miles Davis's composition "Flamenco Sketches" (on which Evans played piano) from *Kind of Blue* (1959). Both songs are based on two chords, sound remarkably similar. Evans and Davis disputed "ownership" of the composition.

p. 109: "I can think about nothing now but power..." comes from *Unforgiving Years*, a novel by Victor Serge, born Victor Lvovich Kibalchich.

p. 112: John C. Stennis was a racist prosecutor (see: Brown v. Mississippi, 1936) and became a pro-segregation U.S. Senator from Mississippi who served in the Senate from 1947 to 1989. Stennis opposed all civil rights legislation in the 50s and 60s though his racism softened somewhat in the 1980s. In 60 years of public life, Stennis never lost an election. James Baldwin, *No Name in the Street*, in *Collected Essays*, p. 433.

p. 114: "The Original Fables of Faubus." *Charles Mingus Presents Charles Mingus*, Candid, 1960. OG Maco, "You Guessed It," 2014. Richard B. Russell, Southern Bloc US Senator from Georgia (1933 – 1971). Dannie Richmond was the drummer in Charles Mingus's groups from 1956 to 1977. No Noise is Garion Morgan, dancer in the short film, *Turf Feinz*.

p. 115: Statement by Richard B. Russell is found in Jason Morgan Ward's *Defending White Democracy: The Making of a Segregationist Movement & the Remaking of*

Politics, 1936-1965, North Carolina University Press, 2011.

p. 118: Saul Bellow's *Herzog*, 1964.

p. 122: Reference to "Antonio" refers to "Fragments of an Opera," (in *Later Poems: Selected and New 1971–2012*) the last poem written by Adrienne Rich. The line "enough, I've taken Antonio [Gramsci] as far as he can go" comes from an e-mail to me dated March 12, 2012.

CORRECTION: WESTERN METAPHYSICS (PLATO'S CAVE) REVISED IN INCOGNITO'S "BABY IT'S ALRIGHT"

p. 147: "Baby It's Alright." On Incognito's album *Eleven*, 2006. Vocals by Imaani.

ACKNOWLEDGMENTS

Many thanks to the editors of the following magazines where pieces of this book first appeared: *Kwani?*, *Kweli Journal*, *Brilliant Corners*, *Chicago Quarterly Review*, *Red Wheelbarrow*, *Washington Square*, *Lana Turner*, and *Wasafiri*.

Many thanks, as well, to the Willson Center for the Humanities at the University of Georgia and to the Hutchins / W.E.B. Du Bois Institute at Harvard University for providing space and time that allowed this book to find its shape.

Special thanks to: Daniel Halpern and Stephanie Stio for their work with the National Poetry Series and to the generous donors whose funding makes the series possible; Rebecca Wolff, Jessica Puglisi, Paul Legault, and Fence Books for giving the book a home; to Khaled Mattawa and Cathy Hong for reading the book in advance of its publication; finally, to John Keene for selecting the manuscript for inclusion in the NPS.

ED PAVLIĆ'S new books are *Let's Let That Are Not Yet: Inferno* (National Poetry Series, Fence Books, 2015) and *Who Can Afford to Improvise?: James Baldwin and Black Music, the Lyric and the Listeners* (Fordham University Press, 2015). Recent works are *Visiting Hours at the Color Line* (National Poetry Series, Milkweed Editions, 2013), *But Here Are Small Clear Refractions* (Achebe Center, 2009, Kwani Trust, 2013) and *Winners Have Yet to be Announced: A Song for Donny Hathaway* (University of Georgia Press, 2008). His other books are *Paraph of Bone & Other Kinds of Blue* (Copper Canyon, 2001), *Crossroads Modernism: Descent and Emergence in African American Literary Culture* (University of Minnesota Press, 2002), and *Labors Lost Left Unfinished* (University Press of New England / Sheep Meadow Press, 2006).

His prizes include the National Poetry Series Open Competition (2012, 2014), the *The American Poetry Review* / Honickman First Book Prize (2001), the Writer of the Year Award from the Georgia Writer's Association (2009), and the Darwin Turner Memorial Award from *African American Review* (1997). He has had fellowships from The MacDowell Colony, Bread Loaf, The Vermont Studio Center, The Willson Center for the Humanities, and the W.E.B. Du Bois Institute at Harvard University. He teaches at the University of Georgia and lives in Athens, Georgia.

ALSO BY ED PAVLIĆ

Who Can Afford to Improvise?:
James Baldwin and Black Music, the Lyric and the Listeners

Visiting Hours at the Color Line

But Here Are Small Clear Refractions

Winners Have Yet to Be Announced:
A Song for Donny Hathaway

Labors Lost Left Unfinished

Crossroads Modernism:
Descent and Emergence in African American Literary Culture

Paraph of Bone & Other Kinds of Blue